Artist to ARTIST

Inspiration & Advice from Artists Past & Present

Artist to ARTIST

Inspiration & Advice from Artists Past & Present

COMPILED BY CLINT BROWN

JACKSON CREEK PRESS ■ CORVALLIS OREGON

PN
6084
A8
B76
1998

Cover and book design by Cheryl McLean.
Cover art: Michelangelo Buonarroti, Creation of Adam,
Sistine Chapel, Vatican Palace, Vatican State.
Photograph courtesy of Scala/Art Resource, New York.

JACKSON CREEK PRESS
2150 Jackson Creek Drive
Corvallis, Oregon 97330
541-752-4666 voice & fax
JacksonCrk@aol.com

Jackson Creek Press books are distributed to the trade by Ingram Books, Bookpeople, Sunbelt Publications, and Far West Book Service, among other jobbers and wholesalers. For personal orders contact the publisher.

Library of Congress Cataloging in Publication Data
Brown, Clint
    Artist to artist: inspiration and advice from artists past and present / Clint Brown, ed.
        p.   cm.
    ISBN 0-943097-04-5 (paper) : $14.95   ISBN 0-943097-05-3 (cloth) : $24.95
    I. Title.
                                                                CIP

Printed in the U.S.A.

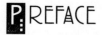# PREFACE

As visual artists, we know that images hold tremendous power. As an educator, I've realized that both words and images are capable of magic, of packaging and storing information about our inner feelings or the outside world. Both can transcend time and space to penetrate minds and seep into souls. Although my primary interest is with the nonverbal communicative power of visual imagery, the words of other artists have moved me deeply, from the earliest days of my study to become an artist—what they have said about art, about living life as an artist, about their passion for creating art.

Their words hold many truths for today's artists and for anyone with an interest in or passion for art. We can follow the advice of Leonardo or Delacroix or Degas. We can be reassured by artists whose own infatuation with color or love of nature mirrors our own. We can be emboldened by Gauguin, who tells us, "There is no such thing as exaggerated art," and heartened by van Gogh's words: "If you hear a voice within you saying, 'You are not a painter,' then by all means paint, boy, and that voice will be silenced."

Jim Dine once said, "My real ancestors are artists of the past. I am comforted and excited and soothed and inspired by them."

When we are discouraged or depressed, it helps to know that some of the most revered artists of our age have experienced the same self-doubts—yet triumphed through their tenacity and unwillingness to surrender to the uncertainty. "I like to start working when it's almost too late," Robert Rauschenberg said, "when nothing else helps . . . . It's then that I find myself in another state, quite outside of myself, and when that happens, there's such a joy!" Or consider Suzanne Valadon, who said, "I paint with the stubbornness I need for living."

When we feel our isolation, Franz Kline reminds us, "You are not alone. There is no way to be alone."

Perhaps most important, the words in these pages form a dialogue that spans distance and time—a rich legacy from artist to artist.

This collection grew out of an informal inquiry into the broad subjects of drawing and the creative process. I wanted to understand how other visual artists thought about creativity—from the old masters of the past to the avant garde artists of the current century. My interests expanded as my reading broadened beyond the initial two subjects. Over the past several years, I gleaned words of inspiration and advice, cynicism and hope, humor and pathos, which I often shared with my students. I found that these brief but often poignant comments could help younger artists see how they fit within the larger community and tradition of artists.

Although I made some effort to seek out the insights of a wide range of artists, I must acknowledge that the emphasis lies with Western art and traditions, more by accident than design. My readings were far from systematic and followed the meandering paths of my own interests.

The artists' statements are grouped together under topical headings, arranged alphabetically, as listed in the table of contents. An index allows you to seek out the words of individual artists.

I consider this a work in progress, one that will continue to grow as my reading expands. As you pursue your own reading, use the blank pages at the back of this book to add new discoveries and insights.

Instead of reading the text as a linear narrative, from cover to cover, think of it more as a mosaic of ideas, some harmonious, some dissonant, each adding something to the whole. You will find statements that seem to echo one another and others that stand at opposing sides of an issue. Some of the artists strive to explain their work—or the importance of art itself—and others acknowledge the futility of such efforts. As Picasso said, "Why not try to understand the song of a bird?"

Whether you feel, like Van Gogh, that you "chose the dog's path through life," or like Alice Neel, who said, "The minute I sat in front of a canvas, I was happy," I think you will find a good many statements that strike a chord in harmony with your own beliefs. Other statements may spark new creative possibilities. In the process, I'm sure you will experience a sense of fellowship and affirmation as an artist.

ACKNOWLEDGMENTS

I first need to acknowledge that all the visual artists included in this text have enriched my life without ever speaking a word. Their art work and their dedication to creating art have provided inspiration for my own endeavors. Still, what so many artists—past and present—have expressed verbally has added to my visual experience.

I would also like to acknowledge that the words quoted here have come from a broad range of sources: historical texts, art criticism, biographies of artists, collections of interviews, magazine articles, exhibition catalogs, newspaper reviews, and others. Several of my colleagues who knew of my interest in quotations shared those that had particular significance to them. Thank you.

Because most of the statements in this text are very short and footnoting would have taken up nearly as much space as the quotation itself, I chose to let the statements stand on their own. Rather than change the look and feel of the book into that of a reference source, I preferred text that allows artists to carry on a dialogue across time and cultures.

The artwork appearing in these pages was graciously provided by a number of individuals and collections. I would especially like to thank my colleague and friend, Dr. Gordon Gilkey, the director and founder of the Vivian and Gordon Gilkey Graphic Arts Collection at the Portland Art Museum; his generosity is much appreciated. My thanks, also, to artists George Green and Martha Mayer Erlebacher, who graciously consented to let their work appear alongside their inspiring words to fellow artists.

I would also like to give a very special thanks to my wife, Cheryl McLean, who is both my "in-house editor" and the production designer for Jackson Creek Press. Without her patience and professional experience, this text would not exist. It is to her and our daughter, Cassidy, that I would like to dedicate this book.

CONTENTS

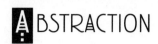BSTRACTION

Abstract means literally to draw from or separate. In this sense every artist is abstract.
        — RICHARD DIEBENKORN
         1922–1993

What goes on in abstract art is the proclaiming of aesthetic principles. . . . It is in our own time that we have become aware of pure aesthetic considerations. Art never can be imitation.
        — HANS HOFMANN
         1880–1966

> *It is surprising to me how many people separate the objective from the abstract. Objective painting is not good painting unless it is good in the abstract sense.*
>   — GEORGIA O'KEEFFE
>   *1887–1986*

To abstract is to draw out the essence of a matter. To abstract in art is to separate certain fundamentals from irrelevant material which surrounds them.
        — BEN SHAHN
         1898–1969

What does that represent? There was never any question in plastic art, in poetry, in music, of representing anything. It is a matter of making something beautiful, moving, or dramatic—this is by no means the same thing.
        — FERNAND LÉGER
         1881–1955

ABSTRACTION

The painter can and must abstract from many details in creating his painting. Every good composition is above all a work of abstraction. All good painters know this. But the painter cannot dispense with subjects altogether without his work suffering impoverishment.　　　　— DIEGO RIVERA
1886–1957

When you see a fish you don't think of its scales, do you? You think of its speed, its floating, flashing body seen through the water. Well, I've tried to express just that. If I made fins and eyes and scales, I would arrest its movement, give a pattern or shape of reality. I want just the flash of its spirit.
　　　　　　　　　　　　　　— CONSTANTIN BRANCUSI
1876–1957

'Realism' has been abandoned in the search for reality: the 'principal objective' of abstract art is precisely this reality.
　　　　　　　　　　　　　　— BEN NICHOLSON
1894–1982

The trouble with recognizable art is that it excludes too much. I want my work to include more. And 'more' also comprises one's doubts about the object, plus the problem, the dilemma of recognizing it.　　　　　　　　　　— PHILIP GUSTON
1913–1980

All painting—the painting of the past as well as of the present— shows us that its essential plastic means we are only line and color.
　　　　　　　　　　　　　　— PIET MONDRIAN
1872–1944

Abstraction is an esoteric language.

— ERIC FISCHL
1948–

What I mean by 'abstract' is something which comes to life spontaneously through a gamut of contrasts, plastic at the same time as psychic, and pervades both the picture and the eye of the spectator with conceptions of new and unfamiliar elements. . . .

— MARC CHAGALL
1889–1985

I think painting is a duality and that abstract painting is an entirely aesthetic thing. It always remains on one level. It is only really interesting in the beauty of its patterns or its shapes.

— FRANCIS BACON
1909–1992

You have to have time to be sorry for yourself to be a good Abstract Expressionist.

— ROBERT RAUSCHENBERG
1925–

Abstract expressionism was the first American art that was filled with anger as well as beauty.

— ROBERT MOTHERWELL
1915–1991

ABSTRACTION

Of course all painting, no matter what you're painting, is abstract in that it's got to be organised.

— DAVID HOCKNEY
1937–

Don't copy nature too much. Art is an abstraction.

— PAUL GAUGUIN
1848–1903

The more abstract is form, the more clear and direct is its appeal.

— WASSILY KANDINSKY
1866–1944

So now the floodgates are open to the delight of pure form, whatever its origin. Anything goes.

— PHILIP JOHNSON
1900–1964

In principle any abstraction of the object is allowed which has a sufficiently strong creative power behind it.

— MAX BECKMANN
1884–1950

There is no abstract art. You must always start with something.

— PABLO PICASSO
1881–1973

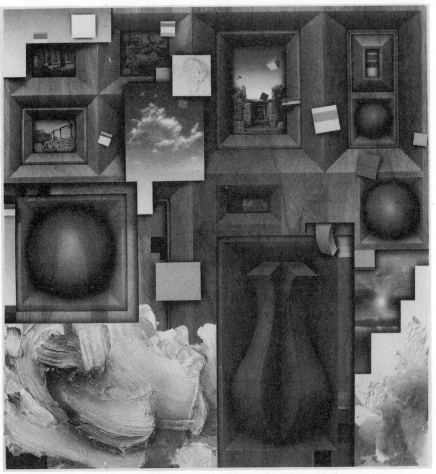

A Will to Order: The Containment of Entropy ▪ *George Green*
Acrylic on Birch, 56" x 53.5", 1998, courtesy of the artist.

*If you make pictures you are bound to be
an abstract painter on some level.*

— GEORGE GREEN
1943–

DVICE

Look at life with the eyes of a child.

— HENRI MATISSE
1869–1954

Be guided by feelings alone. . . . Before any site and any object, abandon yourself to your first impression. If you have really been touched, you will convey to others the sincerity of your emotion.

— JEAN-BAPTIST-CAMILLE COROT
1796–1875

When you paint, try to put down exactly what you see. Whatever else you have to offer will come out anyway.

— WINSLOW HOMER
1836–1910

A young artist must forget painting when he paints. That's the only way he will do original work. To blossom forth, a work of art must ignore or rather forget all the rules.

— PABLO PICASSO
1881–1973

*Take something. Do something to it.
Do something else to it.*

— JASPER JOHNS
1930–

Create like a god, command like a king, work like a slave.

— CONSTANTIN BRANCUSI
1876–1957

Do not strive to be a modern artist: it's the one thing
unfortunately you can't help being.   — SALVADOR DALI
1904–1989

Make a drawing, begin it again, trace it; begin it again and
trace it again.   — EDGAR DEGAS
1834–1917

For this reason take care: never be without your little pad.
Watch the quick motion men make without thinking,
especially under the influence of some strong frame of mind.
Take note of them, sketch them in your pad.
    — LEONARDO DA VINCI
1452–1519

Develop your visual memory. Draw everything you have drawn
from the model from memory as well.   — ROBERT HENRI
1865–1929

But after all, the only principle in art is to copy what you see.
Dealers in aesthetics to the contrary, every other method is fatal.
    — AUGUSTE RODIN
1840–1917

Do not finish your work too much.   — PAUL GAUGUIN
1848–1903

If you hear a voice within you saying, 'You are not a painter,'
then by all means paint, boy, and that voice will be silenced.
    — VINCENT VAN GOGH
1853–1890

ADVICE

An artist, under pain of oblivion, must have confidence in himself, and listen only to his real master: Nature.

— PIERRE AUGUSTE RENOIR
1841–1919

Early on get rid of the idea of rejection, so that you can receive rejection over and over again.

— GEORGE GREEN
1943–

There is only one true thing: instantly paint what you see. When you've got it, you've got it. When you haven't, you begin again. All the rest is humbug.

— ÉDOUARD MANET
1832–1883

Painting isn't a question of sensibility; it's a matter of seizing the power, taking over from nature, not expecting her to supply you with information and good advice.

— PABLO PICASSO
1881–1973

If you want to be a painter never look at pictures.

— WINSLOW HOMER
1836–1910

In the arts there are many right answers. I've learned over the years that when you get a clue to another possibility to follow it through. . . . Ultimately, my hope is to amaze myself.

— JERRY UELSMANN
1934–

The secret is to follow the advice the masters give you in their works while doing something different from them.

— EDGAR DEGAS
1834–1917

Look at nature, work independently, and solve your own
problems. — WINSLOW HOMER
1836–1910

No, the thing to do is try to make a painting that will be alive
in your own lifetime. . . . After thirty or forty years the painting
dies, loses its aura, its emanation, whatever you want to call it.
And then it is either forgotten or else it enters into the
purgatory of art history. But that's all just luck.
—MARCEL DUCHAMP
1887–1968

In matters of art one's state of mind is three-quarters of what
counts, so it has to be carefully nurtured if you want to do
something great and lasting. — PAUL GAUGUIN
1848–1903

When you paint look at your work in a mirror; when you see it
reversed, it will appear to you like some other painter's work
and you will be a better judge of its faults.
— LEONARDO DA VINCI
1452–1519

One must act in painting as in life, directly. . . .
— PABLO PICASSO
1881–1973

*What experience has shown me is that it
takes your life to become an artist.*
— ERIC FISCHL
1948–

ART—WHAT IS IT?

We've let anthropologists, philosophers, historians, connoisseurs, mercenaries, and everybody else tell us what art is or what it should be. I think we ought to very simply let it be what the artist says it is.
— DAVID SMITH
1906–1965

The word 'art' interests me very much. If it comes from Sanskrit, as I've heard, it signifies 'making.'
— MARCEL DUCHAMP
1887–1968

Art is one of the dirtiest words in our language; it's mucked up with all kinds of meanings. There's the art of plumbing, there's the art of almost anything that you can say. My own sense of it is that it means something very rare, an extraordinary achievement. It's not delivered like the morning paper, it has to be stolen from Mount Olympus.
— WAYNE THIEBAUD
1920–

True art is made noble and religious by the mind producing it . . . the endeavor to create something perfect, for God is perfection, and whoever strives after perfection is striving for something divine.
— MICHELANGELO BUONARROTI
1475–1564

Art is limited to the infinite, and beginning there cannot progress.
— JAMES ABBOT MCNEILL WHISTLER
1834–1903

Works of art are made of feeling, concept, and material.
— KENNETH MARTIN
1905–1984

Fine art is that in which the hand, the head and the heart of man go together. — JOHN RUSKIN
1819–1900

I think of art as a glue, a cultural and social glue. It's one of the means that has served to show us the things we believe in and the things we celebrate; it has served to reinforce our relationship to each other. — ERIC FISCHL
1948–

Art is love.
— HOLMAN HUNT
1827–1910

Art is nothing but humanized science. — GINO SEVERINI
1883–1966

Art disturbs, science reassures. — GEORGES BRAQUE
1882–1963

Cold exactitude is not art; ingenious artifice, when it pleases or when it expresses, is art itself. — EUGÈNE DELACROIX
1796–1863

Art does not reproduce the visible, rather, it makes visible.
— PAUL KLEE
1879–1940

What I dream of is an art of balance, of purity and serenity, devoid of troubling or depressing subject matter, an art which could be for every mental worker, for the businessman as well as the man of letters, for example, a soothing, calming influence on the mind, something like a good armchair which provides relaxation from physical fatigue.

— HENRI MATISSE
1869–1954

Art is really a battle.

— EDGAR DEGAS
1834–1917

I am for an art that is political-erotical-mystical, that does something more than sit on its ass in a museum.

— CLAES OLDENBURG
1929–

A *work of art is the trace of a magnificent struggle.*

— ROBERT HENRI
1865–1929

Art must always remain earnest. . . . Art must be serious, no sarcasm, comedy. One does not laugh at a loved one.

— ARSHILE GORKY
1904–1948

The task of the artist is to make the human being uncomfortable, and yet we are drawn to a great work by involuntary chemistry, like a hound getting a scent; the dog isn't free, it can't do otherwise, it gets the scent and instinct does the rest.

— LUCIAN FREUD
1922–

Art is an accurate statement of the time in which it was made.
—ROBERT MAPPLETHORPE
1946–1989

Art is either a plagiarist or a revolutionist.   — PAUL GAUGUIN
1848–1903

Art should be independent of all clap-trap—should stand
alone, and appeal to the artistic sense of eye or ear, without
confounding this with emotions entirely foreign to it, as
devotion, pity, love, patriotism and the like. All these have no
kind of concern with it and that is why I insist on calling my
work 'arrangements' and 'harmonies.' Take the picture of my
mother, exhibited at the Royal Academy as an Arrangement in
Grey and Black. Now that is what it is. To me it is interesting
as a picture of my mother; but what can or ought the public to
care about the identity of the portrait?
— JAMES ABBOT MCNEILL WHISTLER
1834–1903

Art is never chaste. We forbid it to the ignorant innocents,
never allow a contact with those not sufficiently prepared. Yes
art is dangerous, and if it is chaste it isn't art.
— PABLO PICASSO
1881–1973

How do I define a work of art? It is not an asset in the stock-
exchange sense, but a man's timid attempt to repeat the miracle
that the simplest peasant girl is capable of at any time, that of
magically producing life out of nothing.
— OSKAR KOKOSCHKA
1886–1980

ART—WHAT IS IT?

Art is an abstraction. Seek it in nature by dreaming in the presence of it. . . .
— PAUL GAUGUIN
1848–1903

Art is an outsider, a gypsy over the face of the earth.
— ROBERT HENRI
1865–1929

Art is a paradox that has no laws to bind it. . . . When art exists it becomes tradition. When it is created, it represents a unity that did not exist before.
— DAVID SMITH
1906–1965

This idea of art for art's sake is a hoax.
— PABLO PICASSO
1881–1973

Art for art's sake is ridiculous. Art is for the sake of one's needs and I don't think one has a distinct art need; rather art is an intersection of many human needs.
— CARL ANDRE
1935–

As for what I'm making now, perhaps it's art; but if it isn't, at least it's something else equally interesting to me!
— GEORGE RICKEY
1907–

Art is a habit-forming drug.
— MARCEL DUCHAMP
1887–1968

Art isn't art until it's sold. Until then it's an obsession and a
storage problem.   —ANONYMOUS

Art is about mystery.   — MARISOL
1930–

. . . art = a mad search for individualism.   — PAUL GAUGUIN
1848–1903

If it looks like art, chances are it's somebody else's art.
         — CHUCK CLOSE
1940–

A work of art must carry in itself its complete significance and
impose it upon the beholder even before he can identify the
subject-matter. . . . I perceive instantly the sentiment which
radiates from it and which is inherent in the composition in
every line and color.   — HENRI MATISSE
1869–1954

*There is no 'must' in art,
because art is free.*
    — WASSILY KANDINSKY
1866–1944

Everyone wants to understand art. Why not try to understand
the songs of a bird?   — PABLO PICASSO
1881–1973

ARTISTS ON ARTISTS

In my opinion painters owe to Giotto, the Florentine painter, exactly the same debt they owe to nature, which constantly serves them as a model and whose finest and most beautiful aspects they are always striving to imitate and reproduce.

— GIORGIO VASARI
1511–1574

Titian: there is true color, there is nature without exaggeration, without forced brilliance! He is exact.

— JEAN-AUGUSTE-DOMINIQUE INGRES
1780–1867

Titian—there is a man whose qualities can be savored by people who are getting old. . . . The painter qualities are carried to the highest point in his work: what he does is done— through and through; when he paints eyes, they are lit with the fire of life.

— EUGÈNE DELACROIX
1796–1863

Caravaggio. He's still as ugly as ever. There are images of his that set you back on your feet. They flatten you like you haven't been flattened for a while. I'm trying to say that he can't be totally appropriated because he says something about the nature of existence which we don't like to acknowledge.

— LEON GOLUB
1922–

Tintoretto attempted to fill the line of Michael Angelo with color, without tracing its principle.

— HENRY FUSELI
1741–1825

The plague had by this time almost died out, so that the survivors, when they met together alive, rejoiced with much delight in one another's company. This led to the formation of a club of painters, sculptors and goldsmiths, the best that were in Rome; and the founder of it was a sculptor with the name of Michel Agnolo . . . he was the most amusing comrade and the heartiest good fellow in the universe. Of all the members of the club, he was the eldest, and yet the youngest from the strength and vigor of his body.   — BENVENUTO CELLINI
1500–1571

And if we now seek the spiritual significance of the technique of Michelangelo we shall find that his sculpture expressed restless energy. . . . To tell the truth, Michelangelo does not, as is often contended, hold a unique place in art. He is the culmination of all Gothic thought.   — AUGUSTE RODIN
1840–1917

Glory to that Homer of painting, to that father of warmth and enthusiasm . . . he really paints men.

— EUGÈNE DELACROIX
1796–1863
on Rubens

To my eye Rubens' colouring is most contemptible. His shadows are a filthy brown somewhat the color of excrement. These are filled with tints and masses of yellow and red. His lights are all the colours of the rainbow, laid on indiscriminately and broken one into another.   — WILLIAM BLAKE
1757–1827

The grand and heroic draftsmen, then, had better be the models, though one's aim be far from heroic and grand. With their august help one learns to lay one's traps and spread one's nets, to snare the subject matter of one's own intuition and life experience, however special and small. — ISABEL BISHOP
1902–
Referring to Rubens, Michelangelo and Raphael

Just because of Rubens I am looking for a blonde model.
— VINCENT VAN GOGH
1853–1890

What an enchanter! . . . By permitting himself everything, he carries you beyond the limit scarcely attained by the greatest painters . . . he overpowers you with all his liberty and boldness. — EUGÈNE DELACROIX
1796–1863
from his journal, on Rubens

One can claim without fear of contradiction that artists as outstandingly gifted as Raphael are not simply men but, if it be allowed to say so, mortal gods, and that those who leave on earth an honored name in the annals of fame may also hope to enjoy in heaven a just reward for their work and talent.
— GIORGIO VASARI
1511–1574

Leonardo da Vinci, the father, the prince and the first of all painters. . . . For myself, I can see only perfection in him; he is my master and my hero. — PIERRE-PAUL PRUD'HON
1758–1823

Leonardo da Vinci, an artist of outstanding physical beauty who displayed infinite grace in everything he did and who cultivated his genius so brilliantly that all problems he studied he solved with ease. He possessed great strength and dexterity; he was a man of regal spirit and tremendous breadth of mind; and his name became so famous that not only was he esteemed during his lifetime but his reputation endured and became even greater after his death. — GIORGIO VASARI
1511–1574

He modifies a face—to reach for the pictorial characters in his case the drama of the humble, the mystery of life itself, rather than the eccentricity or peculiarity of one particular face: He loses a face but gains a great image. — RICO LEBRUN
1900–1964
on Rembrandt

What does this mean 'Would have been,' one of the first Painters of his Age? Albrecht Dürer Is Not would have been.
— WILLIAM BLAKE
1757–1827

Let us not admire Rembrandt and the others through thick and thin; let us not compare them, either the men or their art, to the divine Raphael and the Italian school: that would be blaspheming.
— JEAN-AUGUSTE-DOMINIQUE INGRES
1780–1867

Ingres did not belong to his age. . . . His works are not true art; for the value of art lies in its power to increase our moral force or establish its heightening influence. — ODILON REDON
1840–1916

Ingres, for me, represents in a feeble degree no more than the beautiful art we lost. Need I tell you I prefer Delacroix with his exaggerations, his mistakes, his visible failures, because he belongs only to himself, because he represents the spirit, the form, the language of his time.   — THEODORE ROUSSEAU
1812–1867

If he had not the strength of plastic rigor Delacroix would have been a Redon.   — ANDRÉ MASSON
1896–1987

His is the greatest palette of France and no one beneath our skies possessed to a greater extent than he both the serene and the pathetic, the vibration of color. We all paint through him.
— PAUL CÉZANNE
1839–1906
on Delacroix

Poor Géricault, I will think of you very often! I imagine that your spirit will often come to hover about my work.
— EUGÈNE DELACROIX
1796–1863
from his journal, upon Géricault's death

Manet did not do the expected. He was a pioneer. He followed his individual whim. Told the public what he wanted it to know, not the time worn things the public already knew and thought it wanted to hear again. The public was very much offended.
— ROBERT HENRI
1865–1929

But the climax of absurdity to which art may be carried when led away from nature by fashion, may be best seen in the works of Boucher. . . .
— JOHN CONSTABLE
1776–1837

Now, Bonnard at times seems styleless. Someone said of him that he had the rare ability to forget from one day to another what he had done. He added the next day's experience to it, like a child following a balloon.
— FRANZ KLINE
1910–1962

Renoir had not only a great interest in human character, in human feeling, but had also a great love for the people he painted.
— ROBERT HENRI
1865–1929

David and his contemporaries exhibited their stern and heartless petrifactions of men and women—with trees, rocks, tables, and chairs, all equally bound to the ground by a relentless outline and destitute of chiaroscuro, the soul and medium of art.
— JOHN CONSTABLE
1776–1837
on Jacques-Louis David

The painters I like? To mention only contemporaries: Delacroix, Corot, Millet, Rousseau, Courbet are masters. And finally all those who loved and had a strong feeling for nature.
— ALFRED SISLEY
1839–1899

He is the painter of painters.
— ÉDOUARD MANET
1832–1883
on Velázquez

ARTISTS ON ARTISTS

Claude Lorraine is a painter who carried landscape to perfection. . . .

— JOHN CONSTABLE
1776–1837

. . . that little chemist.

— PAUL GAUGUIN
1848–1903
on Seurat

Gauguin is not a seer, he is a schemer. . . .

— PABLO PICASSO
1881–1973

Gauguin is the wolf.

— EDGAR DEGAS
1834–1917
Recounting La Fontaine's fable about the dog and the wolf

Vincent and I don't agree on much, and especially not on painting. . . . he is romantic, whereas I, I am more inclined to a primitive state.

— PAUL GAUGUIN
1848–1903

It may be a point of great pride to have a van Gogh on the living room wall, but the prospects of having van Gogh himself in the living room would put a great many devoted art lovers to rout.

— BEN SHAHN
1898–1969

And van Gogh is one of my great heroes because I think that he was able to be almost literal and yet by the way he put on the paint give you a marvellous vision of the reality of things.

— FRANCIS BACON
1909–1992

. . . the artists I'm interested in who are figurative artists are
Giacometti, Balthus, Kitaj, and Lucian Freud. Balthus is the
greatest muse. Or I look to the past: Matisse, Picasso, Cézanne.
I go to Cézanne constantly.   — JIM DINE
             1935–

Pissarro was humble and colossal, something like God the Father.
           — PAUL CÉZANNE
            1839–1906

Henry Ossawa Tanner was, probably alone with Duncanson,
the most important Negro artist of the last century.
         — ROMARE BEARDEN
            1912–

I admire the Spanish artists like Zurbarán and Cotan because
they took solid things and gave them the incredible suggestion
of spirit beyond.   — JANET FISH
            1938–

de Kooning's art was appealing to me, because it was involved
with the draughtsmanship of the past, because it was far-
reaching and farsighted, but also because he could really move
paint around.   — JIM DINE
            1935–

I once met de Kooning and he wasn't empty at all, but I always
found his work empty. . . . Jackson Pollock was the most gifted,
and yet, even with him, when I saw his work, I found it to be a
collection of old lace.   — FRANCIS BACON
            1909–1992

It's not just a coincidence that Jackson Pollock was a Westerner, a kind of pioneer person. Pollock and de Kooning were great friends and great foes. The greatest insult that Pollock could give to de Kooning was to say, 'You are nothing but a goddamned European.' Whereas Pollock was a hero like Daniel Boone and a real pioneer, a real American.   — GRACE HARTIGAN
1922–

Marisol's art has always had wit, but she's dead serious. She brings a complexity to her work, which has a sobering gravity. She's an original.   — GEORGE SEGAL
1924–

Duchamp is a one-man movement, but a movement for each person and open to everybody.   — WILLEM DE KOONING
1904–1997

One admires Léger. But machinery created with brush and paint is ridiculous, all the same. . . . I agree with Renoir, who loved everything handmade.   — ROBERT MOTHERWELL
1915–1991

Kandinsky understood 'form' as a form. . . . He wanted his 'music without words.' He wanted to be simple as a child.
— WILLEM DE KOONING
1904–1997

He is always ten years ahead of the rest of us.
— AMEDEO MODIGLIANI
1884–1920
on Picasso

I've mastered drawing and am looking for color: you've mastered color and are looking for drawing.
— PABLO PICASSO
1881–1973
to Matisse

When Picasso does pure painting he is a great artist. When he paints as a cubist, putting one tone next to another, the arrangement of planes is fine and the results very strong. But those who imitate him achieve nothing worthwhile.
— ARISTIDE MAILLOL
1861–1944

How well I remember seeing for the first time Degas's pastels in the window of a picture dealer on the Boulevard Haussmann. I used to go and flatten my nose against that window and absorb all I could of his art. It changed my life.
— MARY CASSATT
1845–1926
on Edgar Degas

I will not admit that a woman can draw so well.
— EDGAR DEGAS
1834–1917
on examining Mary Cassatt's drawings

In terms of both talent and behavior, Degas is a rare example of what an artist should be.
— PAUL GAUGUIN
1848–1903

Expressionism has been important to me, though, especially the paintings of Max Beckmann. When I was an abstract painter, I found Beckmann's *The Departure* interesting, exciting. . . . *The Departure* made me feel how bankrupt abstraction had become. . . . And the range of Beckmann's pictorial language is so great.

— ERIC FISCHL
1948–

The only fellow who really impressed me, the only artist I really liked, who really gave me confidence in my work, is Alexander Calder.

— JEAN TINGUELY
1925–

I think Calder has something very playful in his nature. His playfulness is genuine and important; it comes out in his work.

— GEORGE RICKEY
1907–

His work impressed me, his personality affected me. He talked a great deal about the paint itself, carving the form and imbuing the paint with this sort of life . . . the idea of paint having that power.

— LUCIAN FREUD
1922–
on Francis Bacon

I met Elizabeth Murray. . . . She worked constantly, wouldn't go to meals, lived on Grape Nuts. She was a real artist to me.

— JENNIFER BARTLETT
1941–

I liked Richard Lindner. Since his death, I've become even
more enamoured of his work. He was an artist I could talk to.

— LARRY RIVERS
1923–

Diebenkorn was a very good critic, a very tough critic, tough
on himself, tough on others. He expected the finest.

— WAYNE THIEBAUD
1920–

Schnabel's work just reeks of art sensibility. It's all grand gesture,
very thought-out that way. It's very clever, but in a sense he's just
sort of handed back American painting to Europe.

— ERIC FISCHL
1948–
on Julian Schnabel

Diego and Frida had open house. In that house you'd see a king
and you'd see a laborer. He never made a distinction—never. There
was nothing he wouldn't give you.   — LOUISE NEVELSON
1900–1988
on Diego Rivera and Frida Kahlo

No words can describe the immense tenderness of Diego for
the things which had beauty. . . . He tries to do and have done
what he considers just in life: to work and create.

— FRIDA KAHLO
1920–1954
on her husband, Diego Rivera

Barney was one of those encouraging people; for a young artist to meet a real artist—just knowing him—made you realize that you were an artist. — LARRY POONS
1937–
about Barnett Newman

What I personally garnered from Albers was the absolute urgency of art. The terrible seriousness of it and how central it was to his life. . . . I never really ran into anyone who was so consumed by art. Truly, he was a magnificent teacher.
— WILLIAM BAILEY
1930–

I consider Albers the most important teacher I've ever had, and I'm sure he considered me one of his poorest students.
— ROBERT RAUSCHENBERG
1925–

Of great importance to me was meeting Bob Rauschenberg. He was a Southerner like me, near my own age, and seemed the first completely devoted artist I had known. — JASPER JOHNS
1930–

Without him I would have given up.
— PIERRE AUGUSTE RENOIR
1841–1919
on Monet

He was such a professor that he could have taught stones to draw correctly. — MARY CASSATT
1845–1926
on Pissarro

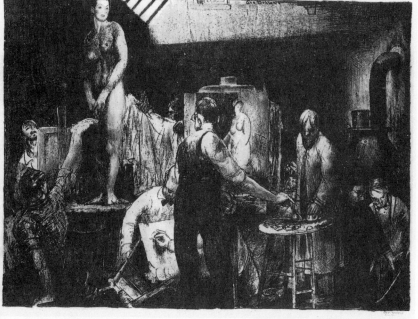

The Life Class ▪ *George Bellows*
Lithograph, 19.4" x 13.9", 1917, courtesy of the Metropolitan Museum of Art, New York.
Purchase, Charles Z. Offin Art Fund Gift, 1978.

*I found myself in my first art school under the direction of
Robert Henri. . . . My life began at this point.*

— GEORGE BELLOWS
1882–1925

BEAUTY

Of which beauty will you speak? There are many: there are a thousand: there is one for every look, for every spirit, adapted to each taste, to each particular constitution.

— EUGÈNE DELACROIX
1798–1863

I hold that the perfection of form and beauty is contained in the sum of all men.

— ALBRECHT DÜRER
1471–1528

Beauty, like truth, is relative to the time when one lives and to the individual who can grasp it. The expression of beauty is in direct ratio to the power of conception the artist has acquired.

— GUSTAVE COURBET
1819–1877

The Platonic ideals were truth, beauty and goodness—not a bad set of ideals to live by. But where's that gone? For thousands of years art was seen as a source of responsible moral and ethical leadership. Today, taking that stance is almost seen as comic.

— JACK BEAL
1931–

I think having land and not ruining it is the most beautiful art that anybody could ever want to own.

— ANDY WARHOL
1927?–1987

It eventually became clear to me that the realistic idea of physical beauty in art which sprang from fifth-century Greece was only a digression from the main world tradition of sculpture.
— HENRY MOORE
1898–1986

W*hat beauty is, I know not, though it adheres to many things.*
— ALBRECHT DÜRER
1471–1528

Come quickly. You mustn't miss the dawn. It will never be just like this again.
— GEORGIA O'KEEFFE
1887–1986
to her house guests at her Abiquin House, 1951

If what a person makes is completely and profoundly right according to his lights then this work contains the whole man.
— RICHARD DIEBENKORN
1922–1993

To the beautiful belongs an endless variety. It is seen not only in symmetry and elegance of form, in youth and health, but is often quite as fully apparent in decrepit old age. It is found in the cottage of the peasant as well as the palace of kings.
— GEORGE CALEB BINGHAM
1811–1879

All art is advertising. It stands for a particular point of view. Art that exploits badness is advertising badness.

— JACK BEAL
1931–

And there are two sorts of beauty; one is the result of instinct, the other of study. A combination of the two, with the resulting modifications, brings with it a very complicated richness, which the art critic ought to try to discover.

— PAUL GAUGUIN
1848–1903

Art is the unceasing effort to compete with the beauty of flowers—and never succeeding.

— MARC CHAGALL
1889–1985

Exuberance is Beauty.
— WILLIAM BLAKE
1757–1827

Philosophers and aestheticians may offer elegant and profound definitions of art and beauty, but for the painter they are all summed up in this phrase: To create a harmony.

— GINO SEVERINI
1883–1966

BEING AN ARTIST

To be an artist is to believe in life.

— HENRY MOORE
1898–1986

The object, which is back of every true work of art, is the attainment of a state of being; a state of high functioning, a more than ordinary moment of existence.

— ROBERT HENRI
1865–1929

If a man devotes himself to art, much evil is avoided that happens otherwise if one is idle.

— ALBRECHT DÜRER
1471–1528

It's a quality of the young to simplify matters. Later a sense of nuance becomes increasingly exaggerated. As one gets older one sees many more paths that could be taken. Artists sense within their own work that kind of swelling of possibilities, which may seem a freedom or a confusion.

— JASPER JOHNS
1930–

I thought you had to give up a lot for art, and you did. It required complete concentration. It also required that whatever money you had had to be put into art materials.

— ALICE NEEL
1900–1984

BEING AN ARTIST

The artist is the man who makes life more interesting or beautiful, more understandable or mysterious, or probably, in the best sense, more wonderful. His trade is to deal with illimitable experience. It is therefore only of importance for the artist to discover whether he be an artist, and it is for society to discover what return it can make of its artist.

— GEORGE BELLOWS
1882–1925

An odd contradiction, if the layman were correct in his unconscious assumption that the artist begins with reality and ends with art: the converse is true—to the degree that this dichotomy has any truth—the artist begins with art, and through it arrives at reality.

— ROBERT MOTHERWELL
1915–1991

Every good artist paints what he is.

— JACKSON POLLOCK
1912–1956

I don't demand that all work be a masterpiece. I think what I am doing is the right thing for me—that is what I am and this is living. It reflects me and I reflect it.

— LOUISE NEVELSON
1900–1988

In the end, I feel that one has to have a bit of neurosis to go on being an artist. A balanced human seldom produces art. It's that imbalance which impels us. . . . The artist lives with anxiety.

— BEVERLY PEPPER
1924–

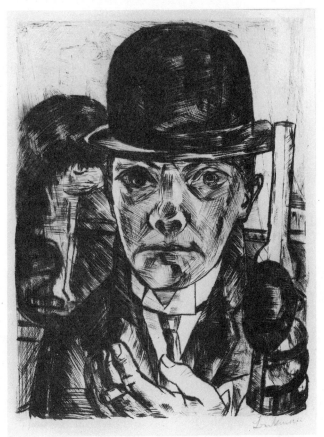

Self-Portrait in Bowler Hat ▪ *Max Beckmann*
Drypoint on laid paper, 13" x 9.75", 1921, courtesy of the Vivian and Gordon Gilkey
Graphic Arts Collection, Portland Art Museum, Portland, Oregon.

Art is creative for the sake of realization, not for
amusement: for transfiguration, not for the sake of
play. It is the quest of our self that drives us along the
eternal and never-ending journey we must all make.

— MAX BECKMANN
1884–1950

The ideal artist is he who knows everything, feels everything, experiences everything, and retains his experience in a spirit of wonder and feeds upon it with creative lust. . . .

— GEORGE BELLOWS
1882–1925

We all name ourselves. We call ourselves artists. Nobody asks us. Nobody says you are or you aren't.

— AD REINHARDT
1913–1967

You find two extremes usually as clichés. One is that, 'Oh, you're a painter? Isn't that wonderful. You're sensitive. You've got all those wonderful, beautiful thoughts.' And the other is, 'You're a little crazy, aren't you?' — ROBERT RAUSCHENBERG
1925–

I feel anyone who does anything great in art and culture is out of control. It is done by people who are possessed. . . . Yet the whole exciting thing about art has to do with being out of control. It has to do with real things. — NANCY GROSSMAN
1940–

Oh, yes. I act like an artist although I'm not one.

— MARCEL DUCHAMP
1887–1968

At the age of six I wanted to be a cook. At seven I wanted to be Napoleon. And my ambition has been growing steadily ever since.

— SALVADOR DALI
1904–1989

THE BUSINESS OF ART

Poor artist! You gave away part of your soul when you painted the picture which you are now trying to dispose of.

— PAUL GAUGUIN
1848–1903

Many critics as well as artists . . . [are] so set in their belief that art is the business supply of reproducing 'things'—they have not learned yet that the 'idea' is what is intended to be represented and the thing is but the material 'used' for its expression.

— ROBERT HENRI
1865–1929

In most cases success equals prison. . . . An artist should never be: prisoner of himself, prisoner of a manner, prisoner of a reputation, prisoner of success.

— HENRI MATISSE
1869–1954

I would sooner look for figs on thistles than for the higher attributes of art from one whose ruling motive in its pursuit is money.

— ASHER B. DURAND
1796–1886

There is too much talk and gossip; pictures are apparently made, like stock-market prices, by competition of people eager for profits. . . . All this traffic sharpens our intelligence and falsifies our judgment.

— EDGAR DEGAS
1834–1917

Living is more a question of what one spends than what one makes.
— MARCEL DUCHAMP
1887–1968

Business art is the step that comes after Art. I started as a commercial artist, and I want to finish as a business artist. After I did the thing called 'art' or whatever it's called, I went into business art. I wanted to be an Art Businessman or a Business Artist.
— ANDY WARHOL
1927?–1987

The ugliest spectacle is that of artists selling themselves. Art as a commodity is an ugly idea. . . . The artist as businessman is uglier than the businessman as artist.
— AD REINHARDT
1913–1967

Art among a religious race produces reliques; among a military one, trophies; among a commercial one, articles of trade.
— HENRY FUSELI
1741–1825

[My art tries] to make observations for which commissioned work generally gives no room and in which fantasy and invention have no limit.
— FRANCISCO DE GOYA
1746–1828

It would be fine if you could get rid of the ridiculous idea that all artists have to be in New York. The current setup does not allow for unique identities to manifest themselves.
— ERIC FISCHL
1948–

The museums of the country are run by boards of trustees which are self-perpetuating. They're there strictly because they're wealthy and that is a dictatorship by a very small minority of the country over the rest of the country.

— CARL ANDRE
1935–

My God! How terrible these money questions are for an artist!

— PAUL GAUGUIN
1848–1903

The practice by which a painter exhibits his works to the gaze of his fellow citizens in return for individual remuneration is not new. . . . If the work is poor, the public taste will soon do it justice. And the author, reaping neither glory nor fortune, will learn by hard experience how to correct his mistakes and capture the attention of the spectator with happier ideas.

— JACQUES-LOUIS DAVID
1748–1825

The exhibition has now become no more than a bazaar where mediocrity spreads itself out with impudence. The exhibitions are useless and dangerous. . . . they ought to be abolished.

— JEAN-AUGUSTE-DOMINIQUE INGRES
1780–1867

. . . one doesn't really work for oneself. That's a myth. Artists have to show their work. It doesn't mean they have to sell it, or peddle it, or use it for anything, but they have to show it.

— AD REINHARDT
1913–1967

I regard it as a waste of time to think 'only' of selling: one forgets one's art and exaggerates one's value.

— CAMILLE PISSARRO
1830–1903

Museums are just a lot of lies, and the people who make art their business are mostly imposters.

— PABLO PICASSO
1881–1973

O painter, take care lest the greed for gain prove a stronger incentive than renown in art, for to gain this renown is a far greater thing than is the renown of riches.

— LEONARDO DA VINCI
1452–1519

Success is what sells.

— ANDY WARHOL
1927?–1987

Painting is a funny business.

— J.M.W. TURNER
1775–1851

COLOR

Color is my day long obsession, joy and torment.

— CLAUDE MONET
1840–1926

I want to paint men and women with that something of the external which the halo used to symbolize, and which we now seek to give by the actual radiance and vibrancy of our colorings.

— VINCENT VAN GOGH
1853–1890

Oh yes! He loved yellow, did good Vincent. . . . When the two of us were together in Arles, both of us insane, and constantly at war over beautiful colors, I adored red; where could I find a perfect vermilion?

— PAUL GAUGUIN
1848–1903
on Vincent van Gogh

There is a logic to color, and it is with this alone and not with the logic of the brain, that the painter should conform.

— PAUL CÉZANNE
1839–1906

When I haven't any blue I use red.

— PABLO PICASSO
1881–1973

COLOR

The chief aim of color should be to serve expression as well as possible. . . . I discover the quality of colors in a purely instinctive way. . . . My choice of color does not rest on any scientific theory; it is based on observation, on feeling, on the very nature of each experience.
— HENRI MATISSE
1869–1954

. . . instead of trying to reproduce exactly what I have before my eyes, I use color more arbitrarily so as to express myself forcibly.
— VINCENT VAN GOGH
1853–1890

Why do two colors, put one next to the other, sing? Can one really explain this? No.
— PABLO PICASSO
1881–1973

Color is like music. The palette is an instrument that can be orchestrated to build form.
— JOHN SLOAN
1871–1951

Color is the keyboard, the eyes are the hammers, the soul is the piano with many strings. The artist is the hand that plays, touching one or the other purposively, to cause vibrations in the soul.
— WASSILY KANDINSKY
1866–1944

Color which, like music, is a matter of vibrations, reaches what is most general and therefore most undefinable in nature: its inner power. . . .
— PAUL GAUGUIN
1848–1903

Harmony is the analogy of contrary and of similar elements of
tone, of color, and of line, conditioned by the dominant key,
and under the influence of a particular light, in gay, calm, or
sad combinations. — GEORGES SEURAT
1859–1891

> *I*t is not pure fantasy to say that the color
> red is like the sound of a trumpet.
> — JOYCE CAREY
> *1888–1957*

Truly color is vice! Of course, it can be, and has the right to be
one of the finest virtues. Controlled by the strong hand and
careful guidance of her Master drawing, color is a splendid
Mistress, with a mate worthy of herself, her lover, but her
Master likewise, the most magnificent Mistress possible, and
the result is evident in all the glorious things that spring from
their union. — JAMES ABBOT MCNEILL WHISTLER
1834–1903

Silver white, chrome yellow, Naples yellow, ochre, raw sienna,
vermilion, rose lake, Veronese green, viridian, cobalt blue,
ultramarine blue. Palette knife, scraper, oil turpentine—
everything necessary for painting. The yellow ochre, Naples
yellow and sienna earth are intermediate tones only, and can be
omitted since their equivalent can be made with other colors.
Brushes made of marten hair: flat silk brushes.
— PIERRE AUGUSTE RENOIR
1841–1919
from the artist's notes describing his palette

I have felt a certain power of color awakening in me.

— VINCENT VAN GOGH
1853–1890

The first colors that made a strong impression on me were bright, juicy green, white, carmine red, black and yellow ochre. These memories go back to the third year of my life.

— WASSILY KANDINSKY
1866–1944

Color, as the strange and magnificent expression of the inscrutable spectrum of Eternity, is beautiful and important to me as a painter; I use it to enrich the canvas and to probe more deeply into the object. Color also decided, to a certain extent, my spiritual outlook, but it is subordinated to light and, above all, to the treatment of form.

— MAX BECKMANN
1884–1950

Drawing and painting are no longer different factors: as one paints one draws: the more harmony there is in the colors the more precise drawing becomes. . . . When the color is at its richest, form is at its fullest.

— PAUL CÉZANNE
1839–1906

When you cover a surface with colors, you must be able to keep the game going indefinitely, continually to find new combinations of colors which will answer to the demands for emotional expression.

— PIERRE BONNARD
1867–1947

Color! What a deep and mysterious language, the language of dreams.
— PAUL GAUGUIN
1848–1903

To exaggerate the fairness of the hair, I come even to orange tones, chromes, and pale lemon yellow. Beyond the head, instead of painting the banal wall of the mean room, I paint infinity, I make a plain background of the richest intensest blue that I can contrive, and by this simple combination of the bright head against the rich blue background, I get a mysterious effect, like a star in the depths of an azure sky.
— VINCENT VAN GOGH
1853–1890

Color possesses me. I don't have to pursue it. It will possess me always, I know it. That is the meaning of this happy hour: Color and I are one. I am a painter.
— PAUL KLEE
1879–1940

Both harmonies and dissonances of color can produce very pleasurable effects.
— HENRI MATISSE
1869–1954

Of greens seen in the country, that of trees and shrubs will appear darker than the green of fields or meadows.
— LEONARDO DA VINCI
1452–1519

COLOR

Colors in painting are as allurements for persuading the eyes, as the sweetness of meter is in poetry. — NICOLAS POUSSIN
1594–1665

You will understand that I limited myself to simple colors, ocher (red-yellow-brown), cobalt and Prussian blue, Naples yellow, sienna, black and white. . . . I refrained from choosing 'nice' colors. . . . — VINCENT VAN GOGH
1853–1890

If I have painted in light tones it is because it is necessary to paint that way. It wasn't the result of a theory, it was a need which was in the air, in everybody's mind, unconsciously, not just in my mind only. — PIERRE AUGUSTE RENOIR
1841–1919

I have always felt that in order to be a good painter one should be color-blind, because color doesn't have to be seen. It needs only to be felt.
— RICHARD LINDNER
1901–1978

Colors, like features, follow the changes of the emotions.
— PABLO PICASSO
1881–1973

Isn't gray a color, too? If I see everything in gray, if within that gray I see all the colors that impress me and that I would like to convey, why should I use another color?

— ALBERTO GIACOMETTI
1901–1966

All colors are the friends of their neighbors and the lovers of their opposites.

— MARC CHAGALL
1889–1985

Painters who are not colorists produce illumination and not painting.

— EUGÈNE DELACROIX
1796–1863

Color is one of the great things in the world that makes it worth living to me and as I have come to think of painting it is my effort to create an equivalent with paint color for the world—life as I see it.

— GEORGIA O'KEEFFE
1887–1986

I've handled color as a man should behave. You may conclude that I consider ethics and aesthetics as one.

— JOSEF ALBERS
1888–1976

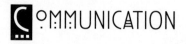OMMUNICATION

Art addresses itself to the mind and not to the eyes.
— JEAN DUBUFFET
1901–1985

What the artist must aim at above all else is this: to produce, by any process whatever, a work which by the life and humanity emanating from it communicates to the beholder. . . .
— MEDARDO ROSSO
1858–1928

I want every man to understand me—without that profundity fashionable these days, without those depths which demand a veritable diving outfit stuffed with cabalistic and metaphysical hocus-pocus.
— GEORGE GROSZ
1893–1959

Paintings must be looked at and looked at and looked at. . . . No writing, no talking, no singing, no dancing will explain them.
— CHARLES DEMUTH
1883–1935

The position of the artist is humble. He is essentially a channel.
— PIET MONDRIAN
1872–1944

Some paint comes across directly onto the nervous system and other paint tells you the story in a long diatribe through the brain.

— FRANCIS BACON
1909–1992

Titles have never given a just idea of things; were it otherwise, the work would be superfluous.

— GUSTAVE COURBET
1819–1877

The difference between painting and other forms of creativity like writing or filmmaking is that painting is a preverbal experience. For me great art is art that creates a moment for you, that takes you into a moment before something is resolved, so that you have an experience without the aid of knowing what that experience is without words already formed to describe it.

— ERIC FISCHL
1948–

But it's the physical properties that are paramount—the marks that a person has put down. And those marks have been throughout our history incredibly powerful things. . . . It's that very inappropriateness of art, that it's a shock, that it's something made by human beings and it's not natural, that makes it interesting.

— JENNIFER BARTLETT
1941–

Art is a language, instrument of knowledge, instrument of communication.
— JEAN DUBUFFET
1901–1985

> *To be understood a writer has to explain almost everything. In a painting, a mysterious bridge seems to exist between its painted subjects and the spectator's spirit.*
> — EUGÈNE DELACROIX
> *1796–1863*

I believe only artists truly understand art, because art is best understood by following the visionary path of the creator who produces it. The Philistines will not attempt the projection.
— DAVID SMITH
1906–1965

If you can talk about it, why paint it?
— FRANCIS BACON
1909–1992

See also The Language of Art

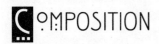
COMPOSITION

And after drawing comes composition. A well-composed
painting is half done.

> — PIERRE BONNARD
> *1867–1947*

Composition is the art of arranging in a decorative manner the
various elements at the painter's disposal for the expression of
his feelings.

> — HENRI MATISSE
> *1869–1954*

It is the medium, or the specific configuration of the medium,
that we call a work of art that brings feeling into being. . . .

> —ROBERT MOTHERWELL
> *1915–1991*

The composition is the organized sum of the interior functions
of every part of the work.

> — WASSILY KANDINSKY
> *1866–1944*

*No matter what the illusion created,
it is a flat canvas and it has to be
organized into shape.*

> — DAVID HOCKNEY
> *1937–*

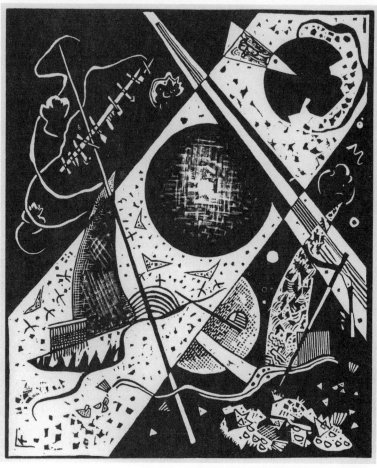

Small Worlds VI ▪ *Wassily Kandinsky*
Woodcut on wove paper, 10.5" x 9.18", 1922, courtesy of the Vivian and Gordon Gilkey
Graphic Arts Collection, Portland Art Museum, Portland, Oregon. 81.81.439.

*The word 'composition' moved me spiritually, and I later
made it my aim in life to paint a 'composition.' It affected
me like a prayer and filled me with awe.*

— WASSILY KANDINSKY
1866–1944

Invention depends altogether upon execution or organization.
— WILLIAM BLAKE
1757–1827

Nature is very rarely right, to such an extent even, that it might
almost be said that nature is usually wrong; that is to say, the
conditions of things that shall bring about the perfection of
harmony worthy a picture is rare, and not common at all.
— JAMES ABBOT MCNEILL WHISTLER
1834–1903

I try to find a compositional structure in the subject itself, in
nature. . . . I rely on the angle where the wall meets the floor as
a constant reference point, and against that I oppose the
movements of the model's limbs.
— PHILIP PEARLSTEIN
1924–

Painting is always strongest when in spite of composition,
color, etc., it appears as a fact, or an inevitability, as opposed to
a souvenir or arrangement.
— ROBERT RAUSCHENBERG
1925–

Height, width, depth are three phenomena which I must
transform into one plane to form the abstract surface of the
picture. . . .
— MAX BECKMANN
1884–1950

COMPOSITION

I therefore wished to compose pictures on canvas similar to
representations on the stage. — WILLIAM HOGARTH
1697–1764

I want a very ordered image, but I want it to come about by
chance. — FRANCIS BACON
1909–1992

*In the arts the way in which an idea is
rendered, and the manner in which it is
expressed, is much more important than the
idea itself. To give a body and a perfect form
to one's thought, this—and only this—is to
be an artist.*

— JACQUES-LOUIS DAVID
1748–1825

I think of the composition of the bodies moving through space
as movements in dance. . . . I just use the model to make
movements, a kind of frozen choreography.

— PHILIP PEARLSTEIN
1924–

Good composition is like a suspension bridge; each line adds strength and takes none away. . . . Making lines run into each other is not composition. There must be motive for the connection. Get the art of controlling the observer, that is composition.

— ROBERT HENRI
1865–1929

Composition, the aim of which should be expression, is modified according to the surface to be covered. If I take a sheet of paper of given size, my drawing will have a necessary relationship to its format. I would not repeat the drawing on another sheet of different proportions, for example, rectangular instead of square. Nor should I be satisfied with a mere enlargement had I to transfer the drawing to a sheet the same shape, but ten times larger . . . one must conceive it anew in order to preserve its expression.

— HENRI MATISSE
1869–1954

Even in front of nature one must compose.
— EDGAR DEGAS
1834–1917

COPYING & IMITATION

Nothing is made with nothing, and the way good inventions are made is to familiarize yourself with those of others. The men who cultivate letters and the arts are all sons of Homer.

— JEAN-AUGUSTE-DOMINIQUE INGRES
1780–1867

The first man to compare the cheeks of a young woman to a rose was obviously a poet; the first to repeat it was possibly an idiot.

— SALVADOR DALI
1904–1989

Do not imitate one another's style. If you do, so far as your art is concerned you will be called a grandson, rather than the son of Nature.

— LEONARDO DA VINCI
1452–1519

Follow the masters! But why should one follow them? The only reason they are masters is that they didn't follow anybody!

— PAUL GAUGUIN
1848–1903

Don't imitate, don't follow the others, or else you will lag behind them.

— JEAN-BAPTIST-CAMILLE COROT
1796–1875

Go and see what others have produced, but never copy anything except nature. You would be trying to enter into a temperament that is not yours and nothing that you would do would have any character.

— PIERRE AUGUSTE RENOIR
1841–1919

When I got to Leeds School of Art in 1919 there were students who'd gone there at fourteen or fifteen as you could in those days, and any excitement or freshness they might have had, had been deadened and killed off by humdrum copying from the antique, just making very careful stump-shaded drawings with no understanding whatever of form.

— HENRY MOORE
1898–1986

Success is dangerous. One begins to copy oneself, and to copy oneself is more dangerous than to copy others. It leads to sterility.

— PABLO PICASSO
1881–1973

When I get my hands on painting materials I don't give a damn about other people's painting: life and me, me and life. In art, every generation must start again afresh.

— MAURICE DE VLAMINCK
1876–1958

COPYING & IMITATION

Make copies, young man, many copies. You can only become a good artist by copying the masters.
— JEAN-AUGUSTE-DOMINIQUE INGRES
1780–1867
to Degas

It is all very well to copy what one sees; it is much better to draw what one no longer sees except in memory. A transformation is effected during which the imagination collaborates with the memory. You reproduce only what has struck you, that is to say, what is necessary. Then your recollections and your fancy are freed from the tyranny which nature exerts. That is why paintings made in this way by a man with a trained memory, one who is well acquainted both with the masters and with the crafts, are almost always remarkable works—witness Delacroix.
— EDGAR DEGAS
1834–1917

If I did what has already been done, I would be a plagiarist and would consider myself unworthy; so I do something different and people call me a scoundrel. I'd rather be a scoundrel than a plagiarist!
— PAUL GAUGUIN
1848–1903

It is better to be nothing than an echo of other painters. The wise man has said: When one follows another, one is always behind.
— JEAN-BAPTIST-CAMILLE COROT
1796–1875

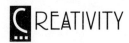

CREATIVITY

Creation is the artist's true function; where there is no creation there is no art.

— HENRI MATISSE
1869–1954

If I create from the heart, nearly everything works; if from the head, almost nothing.

— MARC CHAGALL
1889–1985

The picture is not thought out and determined beforehand, rather while it's being made it follows the mobility of thought.

— PABLO PICASSO
1881–1973

The real artist's work is a surprise to himself.

— ROBERT HENRI
1865–1929

Another thing about creation is that every day it is like it gave birth, and it's always kind of innocent and refreshing. So it's always virginal to me, and it's always a surprise.

— LOUISE NEVELSON
1900–1988

CREATIVITY

I consider a work of art as a product of calculations,
calculations that are frequently unknown to the author himself.
— PABLO PICASSO
1881–1973

The act of creation is a kind of ritual. The origins of art and
human existence lie hidden in this mystery of creation. Human
creativity reaffirms and mystifies the power of 'life.'
—KEITH HARING
1959–1990

You know in my case all painting—and the older I get the
more it becomes so—is an accident. I foresee it, yet I hardly
ever carry it out as I foresee it. It transforms itself by the actual
paint.
— FRANCIS BACON
1909–1992

It is well for young men to have a model, but let them draw the
curtain over it while they are painting. It is better to paint from
memory, for thus your work will be your own. . . .
— PAUL GAUGUIN
1848–1903

One gets into a state of creativity by conscious work.
— HENRI MATISSE
1869–1954

Pictures must be miraculous: the instant one is completed the intimacy between the creation and the creator is ended. He is an outsider. The picture must be for him, as for anyone experiencing it later, a revelation, an unexpected and unprecedented resolution of an eternally familiar need.

— MARK ROTHKO
1903–1970

I have various tricks for myself to actually reach that point of solitary creativity. One of them is pretending that I have an idea. But that trick doesn't survive very long, because I don't really trust ideas—especially good ones. Rather, I put my trust in the materials that confront me, because they put me in touch with the unknown. It's then that I begin to work . . . when I don't have the comfort of sureness and certainty.

— ROBERT RAUSCHENBERG
1925–

In the creative act, the artist goes from intention to realization through a chain of totally subjective reactions. His struggle toward the realization is a series of efforts, pains, satisfactions, refusals, decisions, which also cannot and must not be fully self-conscious, at least on the aesthetic plane.

—MARCEL DUCHAMP
1887–1968

You must create your own world. I'm responsible for my world.

— LOUISE NEVELSON
1900–1988

CREATIVITY

Most art involves a dialogue with the process. Very few painters, sculptors or printmakers would totally previsualize the end result. . . . My point is simply that the creative process can sustain itself throughout the entire celebration of photography.

— JERRY UELSMANN
1934–

An idea is a beginning point and no more. . . . Nothing else matters; creation is all. Have you ever seen a finished picture? A picture or anything else? Woe to you the day it is said that you are finished! To finish a work? To finish a picture? What nonsense! To finish it means to be through with it, to kill it, to rid it of its soul—to give it its final blow; the most unfortunate one for the painter as well as for the picture.

— PABLO PICASSO
1881–1973

The artist begins with a vision—a creative operation requiring an effort. Creativity takes courage.

— HENRI MATISSE
1869–1954

See also Imagination and Inspiration

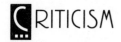

CRITICISM

Nothing is more apt to deceive us more readily than our own judgment of our work. We derive more benefit from having our faults pointed out by our enemies than from hearing the opinions of friends. — LEONARDO DA VINCI
1452–1519

Critics, mathematicians, scientists and busybodies want to classify everything, marking the boundaries and limits. . . . In art, there is room for all possibilities.
— PABLO PICASSO
1881–1973

> *A critic is someone who meddles with something that is none of his business.*
> — PAUL GAUGUIN
> *1848–1903*

I despise the opinion of the press and the so-called critics.
— CLAUDE MONET
1840–1926

It's also always hopeless to talk about painting—one never does anything but talk around it.
— FRANCIS BACON
1909–1992

CRITICISM

Is it not rather that there is no worse influence for certain spirits than the admiration of imbecilic people who know nothing of art?
— PAUL GAUGUIN
1848–1903

At last I could work with complete independence without concerning myself with the eventual judgment of a jury. . . . I began to live.
— MARY CASSATT
1845–1926
said after the Salon rejected her painting

A life passed among pictures makes not a painter—else the policeman in the National Gallery might assert himself. As well allege that he who lives in a library must needs die a poet.
— JAMES ABBOT McNEILL WHISTLER
1834–1903

> *It is a well-known fact that we see the faults in others' works more readily than we do in our own.*
> — LEONARDO DA VINCI
> *1452–1519*

An artist needs the best studio instruction, the most rigorous demands, and the toughest criticism in order to turn up his sensibilities.
— WAYNE THIEBAUD
1920–

Criticism is like many other things, it drags along after what has already been said and doesn't get out of its rut.

— EUGÈNE DELACROIX
1798–1863

After all his literary efforts had come to nought and he had to wear dark glasses, he became an art critic.

— EDVARD MUNCH
1863–1944

People who try to explain pictures are usually barking up the wrong tree.

— PABLO PICASSO
1881–1973

All in all the creative act is not formed by the artist alone; the spectator brings the work in contact with the external world by deciphering and interpreting its inner qualifications and thus adds his contribution to the creative act.

— MARCEL DUCHAMP
1887–1968

The critics say stupid things and we can enjoy them, if we have the legitimate feeling of superiority—the satisfaction of a duty accomplished.

— PAUL GAUGUIN
1848–1903

CRITICISM

To say of a picture, as is often said in its praise, that it shows great and earnest labour is to say that it is incomplete and unfit for view. — JAMES ABBOT MCNEILL WHISTLER
1834–1903

When I used to do the work myself I never read any reviews or any of my own publicity. But then when I sort of stopped doing things and started 'producing' things, I'd want to know what they were saying about them because it wouldn't be anything personal. It was a business decision that I made to start reading reviews of the things I produced, because as the head of a company I felt that I had other people to think about. — ANDY WARHOL
1927?–1987

The sexual, psychological and social readings put on my paintings by anyone, even a professional art writer, are beyond my control and certainly beyond my concern.
— PHILIP PEARLSTEIN
1924–

I've never had an easy relationship with critics. I hold a lot of homicide in my heart. If this was another time, I'd be packing a piece.
— JIM DINE
1935–

None of the art magazines are worth anything. Nobody takes them seriously. . . . I'd rather have one of my pictures reproduced in *Collier's* or *The Saturday Evening Post* than any of the art magazines.

— JACKSON POLLOCK
1912–1956

Slyly, banteringly, but also overbearingly, the critic—the one who does not swallow anything whole, who waits until posterity has consecrated it before . . . howling—is among those who howl their admiration the way they howl their insults: don't be afraid, don't tremble (the beast doesn't have any nails or teeth, or even brain: it is stuffed). . . .

— PAUL GAUGUIN
1848–1903

If on your own or by the criticism of others you discover error in your work, correct it then and there; otherwise in exposing your work to the public, you will expose your error also.

— LEONARDO DA VINCI
1452–1519

We all need critical confrontation of the fullest and most extreme kind that we can get. You can unnecessarily limit yourself by choosing your criticism . . . but how would I feel if Matisse or Morandi or Richard Diebenkorn walked into my studio?

— WAYNE THIEBAUD
1920–

DEATH & DYING

I should like to present myself to the young painters of the year 2000 with the wings of a butterfly.

— PIERRE BONNARD
1867–1947
written shortly before his death

The artist dies, his heirs pounce on his work: they get the copyrights, the auction rooms, the unpublished works, and all the rest of it, until he is completely undressed.

— PAUL GAUGUIN
1848–1903

I want to die as I was born—with nothing. I just want my work to be better. I hope I shall go on painting—in between drinking and gambling—until I drop dead, and I hope I shall drop dead working.

— FRANCIS BACON
1909–1992

Art is man's distinctly human way of fighting death.

— LEONARD BASKIN
1922–

When we are no longer children, we are already dead.

> — CONSTANTIN BRANCUSI
> *1876–1957*

These pictures, which now seem incomprehensible, I
believe, when finally brought together will be more easily
understood—they will deal with love and death.

> — EDVARD MUNCH
> *1863–1944*

When I am dead, let it be said of me: 'He belonged to no
school, to no church, to no institution, to no academy,
least of all to any regime except the regime of liberty.'

> — GUSTAVE COURBET
> *1819–1877*

I remember that one of the art magazines came out with an
issue titled, 'Painting is Dead.' It made painters feel slightly
necrophiliac.

> — ERIC FISCHL
> *1948–*

Between my head and my hand, there is always the face of death.

> — FRANCIS PICABIA
> *1879–1953*

At the moment . . . at this point in my work, I'm looking back.
I think of the nostalgia of life—of time, of death. I look for the
connection with my roots.

> — LARRY RIVERS
> *1923–*
> *at age 55*

DEATH & DYING

Art is an action against death. It is a denial of death.

— JACQUES LIPCHITZ
1891–1973

Disease, insanity and death were the angels which attended my cradle, and since then have followed me throughout my life.

— EDVARD MUNCH
1863–1944

The tomorrow of death is what appeals to me. It is greater than life—stronger than any human ties.

— IVAN ALBRIGHT
1897–1983

Death is the one absolute certainty. Artists know they can't defeat it, but I think that most are very aware of their annihilation—it follows them around like their shadow. . . .

— FRANCIS BACON
1909–1992

I'm not afraid of death but I am afraid of dying. Pain can be alleviated by morphine but the pain of social ostracism cannot be taken away.

— DEREK JARMAN
1942–1994
on being HIV positive

Dying is the most embarrassing thing that can ever happen to you, because someone's got to take care of all of your details.

— ANDY WARHOL
1927?–1987

When it is dark, it seems to me as if I were dying, and I can't think anymore.

— CLAUDE MONET
1840–1926

I am not in love with decay. But I am in love with an object that has experienced some kind of existence.

— RICO LEBRUN
1900–1964

There are times when I can't work, can't do anything. I can't concentrate, I get scattered, feel I'm dying. . . .

— MARY FRANK
1933–

I *hope with all my heart that there will be painting in heaven.*

— JEAN-BAPTIST-CAMILLE COROT
1796–1875
his dying words

I am old and ill, and I have sworn to die painting.

— PAUL CÉZANNE
1839–1906
letter to Emile Bernard, 1906

Every person is a new universe unique with its own laws emphasizing some belief or phase of life immersed in time and rapidly passing by. Death, the great void of life, hangs over everyone.
— ALICE NEEL
1900–1984

A painting is life and a painting is death . . . the picture is our own legacy left by tomorrow's dead for tomorrow's living.
— IVAN ALBRIGHT
1897–1983

When I die I don't want to leave any leftovers. I'd like to disappear. People wouldn't say 'He died today,' they'd say 'He disappeared.' . . . and it would be very glamorous to be reincarnated as a big ring on Elizabeth Taylor's finger.
— ANDY WARHOL
1927?–1987

DESIGN

A designer is a planner with an aesthetic sense.

— BRUNO MUNARI
1907–

Good design, like good painting, cooking, architecture or whatever you like, is a manifestation of the capacity of the human spirit to transcend its limitations.

— GEORGE NELSON
1907–

Good design means as little design as possible.

— DIETER RAMS
1952–

> *Less is more.*
>
> — MIES VAN DER ROHE
> *1886–1969*
>
> *More is less.*
>
> — AD REINHARDT
> *1913–1967*
>
> *Less is a bore.*
>
> — ROBERT VENTURI
> *1925–*

Every human being is a designer.

— NORMAN POTTER
20th century

DESIGN

All we do, almost all the time, is design, for design is basic to all human activity.
— VICTOR PAPANEK
1925–

You have to doubt, all the time, feel unsatisfied until, for some reason, and that is the mystery of the design process, until you feel it (the solution) is the one that is right.
— MARIO BELLINI
1935–

The science of design, or of line-drawing, if you like to use this term, is the source and very essence of painting, sculpture, architecture. . . . Sometimes . . . it seems to me that . . . all the works of the human brain and hand are either design itself or a branch of that art.
— MICHELANGELO BUONARROTI
1475–1564

DOCTRINE: RULES & THEORY

Pictures aren't made out of doctrines. Since the
appearance of impressionism, the official salons, which
used to be brown, have become blue, green and red. . . .
— CLAUDE MONET
1840–1926

*You know it's very hard to maintain a
theory in the face of life that comes
crashing about you.*
— ALICE NEEL
1900–1984

How awful for a painter who loathes apples to have to use
them all the time because they go so well with the cloth. I put
all the things I like in my pictures.
— PABLO PICASSO
1881–1973

In general, young artists today depend less on forbearers (if
any), and are less interested in the categories and limits by
which the art world has been traditionally defined. They are
more interested in what you might call life experience, in
relatively direct transcription of circumstances—political,
sexual, whatever.
— LEON GOLUB
1922–

DOCTRINE: RULES & THEORY

An art of creating . . . is nothing less than a building of a
bastion housed and armed with absolutist beliefs which are
the artist's only weapons. . . . If one accedes to the notion of
an artist as an armored creature engaged in stylistic warfare,
then one must . . . allow for some artists the role of guerrilla
fighters in the struggle.

— LEONARD BASKIN
1922–

*The supreme misfortune is when theory
outstrips performance.*

— LEONARDO DA VINCI
1452–1519

What is to be done about these literary people, who will never
understand that painting is a craft and that the material side
comes first? The ideas come afterwards, when the picture is
finished.

— PIERRE AUGUSTE RENOIR
1841–1919

Real painters understand with a brush in their hand. . . . What
does anyone do with rules? Nothing worthwhile. What's
needed is new, personal sensations; and where to learn those?

— BERTHE MORISOT
1841–1895

*Y*ou come to nature with your own
theories, and she knocks them all flat.
— PIERRE AUGUSTE RENOIR
1841–1919

An art which does not obey fixed and inviolable laws is
the true art, what noise is to sound. . . .
— GINO SEVERINI
1883–1966

One must beware of a formula 'good for everything,' that will
serve to interpret the other arts as well as reality, and that
instead of creating will only produce a style, or rather a
stylization.
— GEORGES BRAQUE
1882–1963

Theories are patterns without value. What counts is action.
— CONSTANTIN BRANCUSI
1876–1957

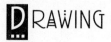RAWING

I sometimes think there is nothing so delightful as drawing.
— Vincent van Gogh
1853–1890

Drawing is the artist's most direct and spontaneous expression, a species of writing: it reveals, better than does painting, his true personality.
— Edgar Degas
1834–1917

Drawing is a kind of hypnotism: one looks in such a way at the model, that he comes and takes a seat on the paper.
— Pablo Picasso
1881–1973

And when you see great academic drawings you realize what achievement they are. . . . It's a touchstone to the poetry of form.
— Wayne Thiebaud
1920–

A critic at my house sees some paintings. Greatly perturbed, he asks for my drawings. My drawings? Never! They are my letters, my secrets.
— Paul Gauguin
1848–1903

Drawing is like making an expressive gesture with the
advantage of permanence. — HENRI MATISSE
1869–1954

I looked at the drawings of the Old Masters from the point of
view of learning what drawing was. — HENRY MOORE
1898–1986

It is a false idea that drawing in itself can be beautiful. It is only
beautiful through the truths and feelings it translates.
— AUGUSTE RODIN
1840–1917

Drawing is the probity of art.
— JEAN-AUGUSTE-DOMINIQUE INGRES
1780–1867

Realize that a drawing is not a copy. It is a construction in very
different materials. A drawing is an invention.
— ROBERT HENRI
1865–1929

Drawing is not form, it is a way of seeing form.
— EDGAR DEGAS
1834–1917

My drawings are done mainly as a help towards making
sculpture—as a means of generating ideas for sculpture,
tapping oneself for the initial ideas; and as a way of sorting out
ideas and developing them. — HENRY MOORE
1898–1986

DRAWING

I have never considered drawing as an exercise of particular dexterity, rather as principally a means of expressing intimate feelings and describing states of mind.   — HENRI MATISSE
1869–1954

It's not just a matter of academic training. You can't understand it without being emotionally involved. It really is a deep, strong, fundamental struggle to understand oneself, as much as to understand what one is drawing.   — HENRY MOORE
1898–1986

To know what you want to draw, you have to begin drawing it.
— PABLO PICASSO
1881–1973

Drawing is not following a line on the model, it is drawing your sense of the thing.   — ROBERT HENRI
1865–1929

Drawing is the basis of art. A bad painter cannot draw. But one who draws well can always paint.

— ARSHILE GORKY
1905–1948

Drawing includes three and a half quarters of the content of painting. . . . Drawing contains everything but hue.
— JEAN-AUGUSTE-DOMINIQUE INGRES
1780–1867

Drawing and color are not separate. In proportion as one paints, one draws. The more harmonious the color, the more the drawing takes shape. When color is at its richest, form is at its fullest; contrasts and tone gradations, that is the secret of drawing and richness of form.

— PAUL CÉZANNE
1839–1906

A drawing must have an expansive force which gives life to the things around it.

— HENRI MATISSE
1869–1954

I have always tried to urge my colleagues to seek for new combinations along the path of draughtsmanship, which I consider a more fruitful field than that of color.

— EDGAR DEGAS
1834–1917

It is not bright colors but good drawing that makes figures beautiful.

— TITIAN
1488–1576

I've always drawn as my exploration of forms and space. . . .

— DAME BARBARA HEPWORTH
1903–1975

Drawing is the most important thing.

— ANTONIO GIACOMETTI
1901–1966

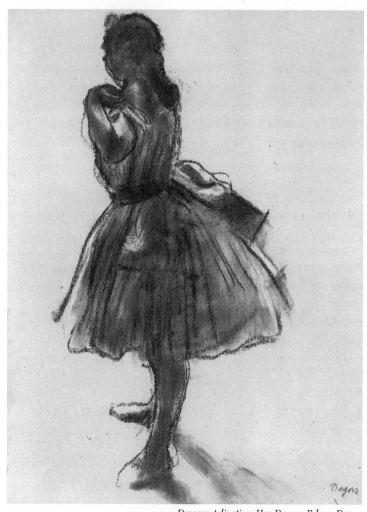

Dancer Adjusting Her Dress ▪ *Edgar Degas*
Pastel on paper, 23.375" x 12", courtesy of the Portland Art Museum,
Portland, Oregon. Bequest of Winslow B. Ayer.

The dancer is only a pretext for a drawing.
— EDGAR DEGAS
1834–1917

A colorist makes his presence known even in a simple charcoal drawing.
— HENRI MATISSE
1869–1954

> *For me, drawing is the great discipline of art.*
> — ALICE NEEL
> *1900–1984*

Drawing is the first of the virtues for a painter. It is everything; a thing well drawn is always well enough painted.
— JEAN-AUGUSTE-DOMINIQUE INGRES
1780–1867

Knowing how to draw is not the same thing as drawing well. . . .
— PAUL GAUGUIN
1848–1903

Facility alone does not produce good drawing.
— HENRY MOORE
1898–1986

The man who has something very definite to say and tries to force the medium to say it will learn how to draw.
— ROBERT HENRI
1865–1929

See also Line and Sketching

EDUCATION & TRAINING

A student should early acquire a knowledge of perspective to enable him to give every object its proper dimensions; then he should have a good master who will gradually teach him a good style of drawing. Next, he should study Nature, in order to confirm and fix in his mind the reason for the rules he has learned; and also give some time to the study of old masters in order to form his eye and judgment so that he may put into practice what he has learned.

— LEONARDO DA VINCI
1452–1519

Certainly we have to fall in line and learn our lesson from the Master. If there is another way it has not been discovered yet. It seems that the line of Culture is continuous, without short cuts, unbroken from the unknown Beginning to the unknown End.

— JOSÉ CLEMENTE OROZCO
1883–1949

The art of the past required the study of the nude, statues, drapery, and the antique, and for this a school was necessary. But nowadays a young artist must study in the fields, in the streets, in the cafes. . . .

— GIOVANNI SEGANTINI
1858–1899

The scholar specialized in any field will find that the more he knows, the more he will have to learn. . . . Art and science mean trying to understand.

— ALBERTO GIACOMETTI
1901–1966

The Louvre is the book in which we learn to read. We must not, however, be satisfied with retaining the beautiful formulas of our illustrious predecessors. Let us go forth to study beautiful nature, let us try to free our minds from them, let us strive to express ourselves according to our personal temperaments.

— PAUL CÉZANNE
1839–1906

But it was at the Louvre that I felt most at home. Friends long vanished. Their prayers, mine. Their canvases light my childish face. Rembrandt captivated me and more than once I stopped before Chardin, Fouquet, Géricault.

— MARC CHAGALL
1889–1985

Let a student enter the school with this advice: No matter how good the school is, his education is in his own hands. All education must be self-education.

— ROBERT HENRI
1865–1929

EDUCATION & TRAINING

It took me twenty years to discover painting: twenty years looking at nature, and above all, going to the Louvre. But when I say discover—! I am still beginning, and I still go on making mistakes.
— PIERRE AUGUSTE RENOIR
1841–1919

I deny that art can be taught, or, in other words, maintain that art is completely individual, and that the talent of each artist is but the result of his own inspiration and his own study of past tradition.
— GUSTAVE COURBET
1819–1877

Schools and things that painters have taught me even keep me from painting as I want to. I decided I was a very stupid fool not to at least paint as I wanted to and say what I wanted to when I painted as that seemed to be the only thing I could do that didn't concern anybody but myself—that was nobody's business but my own.
— GEORGIA O'KEEFFE
1887–1986

I've taught, and the first thing I did when I taught art, was not to teach art. I taught the students to clean their minds, to take that mind and polish it daily, to throw out what they don't need and not to clutter it. . . . Keep it open and keep it empty, so that when you see something, you see it totally.
— LOUISE NEVELSON
1900–1988

Painters must study the universal laws of nature and ponder much on everything.

— LEONARDO DA VINCI
1452–1519

A n artist has to train his responses more than other people do. . . . He has to be as disciplined as a mathematician. Discipline is not a restriction but an aid to freedom. It prepares an artist to choose his own limitations.

— WAYNE THIEBAUD
1920–

The more sublime efforts of art have no effect at all upon uncultivated minds. Fine and delicate taste is the fruit of education and experience.

— JEAN-AUGUSTE-DOMINIQUE INGRES
1780–1867

The public wants to understand and learn in a single day, a single minute, what the artist has spent years learning.

— PAUL GAUGUIN
1848–1903

EDUCATION & TRAINING

Part of the problem is that artists of my generation were not educated. We were not given the equipment because it was generally believed to be irrelevant. Drawing, eye-hand coordination, art history—really fundamental stuff was considered unnecessary.

— ERIC FISCHL
1948–

I think that you should have a good solid thing called drawing. Probably to work with the figure would be the best way to learn that. . . . No art history or aesthetics or any of that, just beautiful drawing. I wouldn't allow them to read any art magazines.

— RICHARD ESTES
1932–

In order to develop skills of looking at painting you have to see different expressions of art from different times and different countries that are addressing different goals. Inevitably there's going to be a drift to the work that you particularly like.

— JENNIFER BARTLETT
1941–

One learns about painting by looking at and imitating other painters. I can't stress enough how important it is, if you are interested at all in painting, to look and to look a great deal at painting. There is no other way to find out about painting.

— FRANK STELLA
1936–

Which teacher is capable of transmitting his personal feelings? One can only take his recipes.

— EUGÈNE DELACROIX
1796–1863

I had this attitude that it was going to take time for my work to grow. I had to develop skills to do what I wanted and I didn't really expect it was going to happen rapidly—a lot of people come out of art school with a nice slick image but not much of their own personality in it. They don't have the time to work the idea through.

— JANET FISH
1938–

I still think that going to school is a much better way to start out as a young artist. . . . I mean, it's very nice to have your lofts first, but it doesn't quite work out that way, because an awful lot of frustration and energy is put into just trying to survive.

— ROBERT RAUSCHENBERG
1925–

For education does not give only knowledge, but taste: it qualifies the feelings as well as the judgment.

— JOYCE CAREY
1888–1957

EDUCATION & TRAINING

The only way to understand painting is to go and look at it.
And if out of a million visitors there is even one to whom art
means something, that is enough to justify museums.

— PIERRE AUGUSTE RENOIR
1841–1919

I like the idea of the museum world and the university-
academic situation where artists talk to each other or where
artists or art students study with artists.

— AD REINHARDT
1913–1967

*One has complexes. One has the art
complex. One goes to the School of Fine
Arts and catches the complexes.*

— JEAN TINGUELY
1925–

There are pictures that manifest education and there are
pictures that manifest love.

— ROBERT HENRI
1865–1929

EXPRESSION & EMOTION

All art, literature and music must be brought forth with your heart's blood. Art is your heart's blood.

— EDVARD MUNCH
1863–1944

There is no such thing as exaggerated art. I even believe that there is salvation only in extreme.

— PAUL GAUGUIN
1848–1903

One never paints violently enough.

— EUGÈNE DELACROIX
1796–1863

What I want is that my picture should evoke nothing but emotion.

— PABLO PICASSO
1881–1973

I want to put strongly and completely all that is necessary, for I think things weakly said might as well not be said at all.

— JEAN-FRANÇOIS MILLET
1814–1875

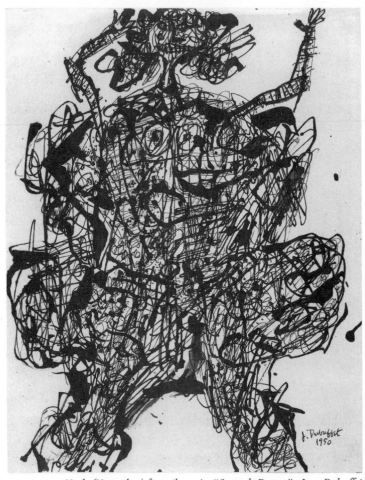

Nude (November) from the series "Corps de Dames" ▪ *Jean Dubuffet*
Pen, reed pen and ink, 10.6" x 8.4", 1950, courtesy of the Museum of Modern Art,
New York. The Joan and Lester Avnet Collection.

*Personally, I believe very much in values of savagery; I
mean: instinct, passion, mood, violence, madness.*

— JEAN DUBUFFET
1901–1985

The deepest and most lifelike emotion has been expressed, and that is the reason they have taken so long to execute.

— REMBRANDT VAN RIJN
1606–1669
Reportedly the only existing written statement Rembrandt made describing his work. From a letter to his patron, Constantijn Huygens

My aim is a continuous, sustained, uncontrived image, motivated by nothing but passion.

— RICO LEBRUN
1900–1964

I have never been able to carry out any work coolly. On the contrary it is done, so to speak, with my own blood. Anyone who looks at my works must be able to sense that.

— KÄTHE KOLLWITZ
1867–1945

I'm not an abstractionist. . . . I'm interested only in expressing basic human emotions.

— MARK ROTHKO
1903–1970

Plastic rigor cannot be replaced by even the richest literary imagination. A painting or sculpture does not have a survival value if it lacks plastic rigor.

— ANDRÉ MASSON
1896–1987

EXPRESSION & EMOTION

Where does the execution of a painting commence and where does it end? At that moment, when the most intense emotions are in fusion in the depths of one's being, when they burst forth and when thought comes up like lava from a volcano, is there not then something like an explosion? The work is created suddenly, brutally if you like, and is not its appearance great, almost superhuman?

— PAUL GAUGUIN
1848–1903

We nearly always live through screens—a screened existence. And I sometimes think, when people say my work looks violent, that perhaps I have from time to time been able to clear away one or two of the veils or screens.

— FRANCIS BACON
1909–1992

Between beauty of expression and power of expression there is a difference of function. The first aims at pleasing the senses, the second has a spiritual vitality which for me is more moving and goes deeper than the senses.

— HENRY MOORE
1898–1986

What measure is there, other than the fact that at 'one' point in your life you trusted a feeling. You have to trust that feeling and then continue trusting yourself.

— PHILIP GUSTON
1913–1980

[The artist should depict] his deepest emotions, his soul, his sorrows and joys . . . to move people intensely, first a few, then more and more. — EDVARD MUNCH
1863–1944

The painter must give a completely free rein to any feeling or sensations he may have and reject nothing to which he is naturally drawn. It is just this self-indulgence which acts for him as the discipline through which he discards what is unessential to him and so crystallizes his tastes.
— LUCIAN FREUD
1922–

The artist is a receptacle for emotions that come from all over the place: from the sky, from the earth, from a scrap of paper, from a passing shape, from a spider's web.
— PABLO PICASSO
1881–1973

What am I in most people's eyes? A nonentity or an eccentric and disagreeable man. . . . I should want my work to show what is in the heart of such an eccentric, of such a nobody.
— VINCENT VAN GOGH
1853–1890

Emotion should not be rendered by an excited trembling; it can neither be added on nor be imitated. It is the seed, the work is the flower. — GEORGES BRAQUE
1882–1963

EXPRESSION & EMOTION

I believe that the great painters, with their intellect as master, have attempted to force the unwilling medium of paint and canvas into a record of their emotions. I find any digression from this large aim leads me to boredom.

— EDWARD HOPPER
1882–1967

I want to do drawings which touch some people. . . . In either figure or landscape I should wish to express, not sentimental melancholy, but serious sorrow.   — VINCENT VAN GOGH
1853–1890

But the artist doesn't look at another artist ever as somebody who's had some kind of experience that he's expressing other than the painting experience. That's for laymen, the idea that an artist expresses some life experience he's had.

— AD REINHARDT
1913–1967

Nature is a mere pretext for a decorative composition, plus sentiment. It suggests emotion, and I translate that emotion into art.   — GEORGES BRAQUE
1882–1963

Expression, to my way of thinking, does not consist of the passion mirrored upon a human face or betrayed by a violent gesture. The whole arrangement of my picture is expressive.

— HENRI MATISSE
1869–1954

Despite any will I may have in the matter, what I express interests me more than my ideas.

— PABLO PICASSO
1881–1973

I think very few people have a natural feeling for painting, and so, of course, they naturally think that painting is an expression of the artist's mood. But it rarely is. Very often he may be in greatest despair and be painting his happiest paintings.

— FRANCIS BACON
1909–1992

*J*ust as Leonardo da Vinci studied human anatomy and dissected corpses, so I try to dissect souls.

— EDVARD MUNCH
1863–1944

I decided that expressionism was a cheap way of getting a reaction—show anybody ripped apart, and you get sympathy. I was deliberately trying to show the human body as whole and relatively healthy.

— PHILIP PEARLSTEIN
1924–

FEAR & DOUBT

When I am halfway there with a painting, it can occasionally be thrilling, and I can stop and say, 'Gee, how lucky I am to be doing this activity that I like to do!' But it happens very rarely; usually it's agony. If it doesn't come out looking agonized, it's because I have a dread of that appearing in the work. I go to great pains to mask it. But the struggle is there. It's the invisible enemy.

— RICHARD DIEBENKORN
1922–1993

I felt so insufficiently equipped, so unprepared, so weak, and at the same time it seemed to me that my reflections on art were correct. I quarrelled with all the world and with myself.

— EDGAR DEGAS
1834–1917

It was always disappointing to see that what I could really master in terms of form boiled down to so little.

— ALBERTO GIACOMETTI
1901–1966

The only sensible way to regard the art life is that it is a privilege you are willing to pay for. . . . You may cite honors and attentions and even money paid, but I would have you note that these were paid a long time after the creator had gone through his struggles.

— ROBERT HENRI
1865–1929

The attacks of which I have been the object have broken the spring of life in me. . . . People don't realize what it feels like to be constantly insulted. — ÉDOUARD MANET
1832–1883

Finishing a painting demands a heart of steel: everything requires a decision, and I find difficulties where I least expect them. . . . It is at such moments that one fully realizes one's own weaknesses. — EUGÈNE DELACROIX
1796–1863

Even at this late date, I go into my studio, and I think 'Is this going to be it? Is it the end?' You see, nearly everything terrorizes me. I think that when an artist loses that terror, he's through.
— ROBERT RAUSCHENBERG
1925–

What still concerns me the most is: am I on the right track, am I making progress, am I making mistakes in art? Such things as the materials, and care in the actual process of painting, and even of preparing the canvas, are the least important. They can always be fixed up, can't they? Whereas art—oh, it's a very awkward and a very awesome thing to go into deeply.
— PAUL GAUGUIN
1848–1903

FEAR & DOUBT

I come into the studio very fearfully. I creep in to see what happened the night before. And the feeling is one of, 'My God, did I do that?'
— PHILIP GUSTON
1913–1980

The feelings of desperation and unhappiness are more useful to an artist than the feeling of contentment, because desperation and unhappiness stretch your whole sensibility.
— FRANCIS BACON
1909–1992

I never know where I am going with a painting. I only know where I've been, and frankly, I believe that every painter is in a state of continual failure. The only constant in a painter's life is failure.
— WILLIAM BAILEY
1930–

I believe in listening to cycles. I listen by not forcing. If I am in a dead working period, I wait, though these periods are hard to deal with. For the future, I'll see what happens. I'll be content if I get started again. If I feel that alive again. If I find myself working with the old intensity again.
— LEE KRASNER
1908–1983

Of course, I don't go into the studio with the idea of 'saying' something—that's ludicrous. What I do is face the blank canvas, which is terrifying. Finally I put a few arbitrary marks on it that start me on some sort of dialogue.
— RICHARD DIEBENKORN
1922–1993

I had wrung impressionism dry and I finally came to the conclusion that I know neither how to paint nor how to draw.

— PIERRE AUGUSTE RENOIR
1841–1919

I assumed that everything would lead to complete failure, but I decided that didn't matter—that would be my life.

— JASPER JOHNS
1930–

I was discouraged about life, discouraged about people being blind, but I don't think I had a day that I ever questioned creativity. There has never been a day like that.

— LOUISE NEVELSON
1900–1988

You see in the past, my needs were very great and my fears were very great and my defenses look like torture. Well I have come to terms with a lot of things, because, when all's said and done, there's really very little one can do about a lot of things. You just accept them. The point is you just have to keep on working and you just have to keep on living. That's the ball game.

— JIM DINE
1935–

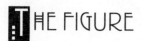HE FIGURE

The sight of a fine human figure is above all things pleasing to us. . . .
— ALBRECHT DÜRER
1471–1528

What interests me most is neither still life nor landscape but the human figure. It is through it that I best succeed in expressing the nearly religious feeling that I have toward life.
— HENRI MATISSE
1869–1954

Nor is there any 'figurative' and 'nonfigurative' art. Everything appears to us in the guise of a figure.
— PABLO PICASSO
1881–1973

The difficulties in drawing the figure— that is, manipulating and using the figure in a composition—are enormous.
— MARTHA MAYER ERLEBACHER
1948–

The construction of the human figure, its tremendous variety of balance, of size, of rhythm, all those things make the human form much more difficult to get right in a drawing than anything else.
— HENRY MOORE
1898–1986

I have saved the figure from its tormented agonized condition given it by expressionistic artists, and the cubist dissectors and distorters of the figure, and at the other extreme, I have rescued it from the pornographers, and their easy exploitations of the figure for its sexual implications.

— PHILIP PEARLSTEIN
1924–

I think that the natural reaction of the artist will be strongly towards bringing man back into focus as the center of importance.

— BEN SHAHN
1898–1969

The figures . . . are not supposed to reveal anything. . . . It's like seeing a stranger in some place like an air terminal for the first time. You look at him, you notice his shoes, his suit, the pin in his lapel, but you don't have any particular feeling about him.

— WAYNE THIEBAUD
1920–

You would hardly believe how difficult it is to place a figure alone on a canvas, and to concentrate all the interest on this single and universal figure and still keep it living and real.

— ÉDOUARD MANET
1832–1883

THE FIGURE

Fit the parts together, one into the other, and build your figure
like a carpenter builds a house. Everything must be
constructed, composed of parts that make a whole. . . .

— HENRI MATISSE
1869–1954

> *The figure is still the only thing I have*
> *faith in in terms of how much*
> *emotion it's charged with and how*
> *much subject matter is there.*
>
> — JIM DINE
> *1935–*

How wrong are those simpletons, of whom the world is full,
who look more at . . . color than at the figures which show
spirit and movement.   — MICHELANGELO BUONARROTI
1475–1564

See also Human Anatomy, The Model, and The Nude

GENDER & RACE

I believe that it is crucial for women artists to situate ourselves
in the context of our own gender, class, and ethnic histories
and struggles rather than in relationship to male histories.

— JUDY CHICAGO
1939–

There's only one thing in life for a woman; it's to be a
mother. . . . A woman artist must be . . . capable of making the
primary sacrifices.

— MARY CASSATT
1844–1926

I don't paint like a woman is supposed to paint. Thank God,
art doesn't bother about things like that.

— ALICE NEEL
1900–1984

True strength is delicate.

— LOUISE NEVELSON
1900–1988

Maybe in that earlier phase I was painting the woman in me.
Art isn't a wholly masculine occupation, you know.

— WILLEM DE KOONING
1904–1997

I find that women can be creative in total isolation. I know
excellent women artists who do original work without any
response to speak of. Maybe they are used to a lack of feedback.
Maybe they are tougher.

— ELAINE DE KOONING
1920–

All artists, Negro and white, have the problem of making a living, of finding a gallery or a place where they can display their work and often with the Negro artist these problems are attenuated.

— ROMARE BEARDEN
1912–

I love to tell a story. The history of the United States fascinates me. . . . The part the Negro has played in all these events has been greatly overlooked. I intend to bring it out.

— JACOB LAWRENCE
1917–

I feel that women 'and men,' but I mean the 'individual,' can be totally feminine and still be totally powerful.

— LOUISE NEVELSON
1900–1988

I don't think the quality of being a good teacher or a good artist has anything to do with sex. I think it's objective: you either are or you aren't.

— ALICE NEEL
1900–1984

At no point do I wish to be in conflict with any man or masculine thought. It doesn't enter my consciousness. I think art is anonymous. It's not competitive with men. It's a complementary contribution.

— DAME BARBARA HEPWORTH
1903–1975

There you are alone in this huge space and you are not conscious of the fact that you have breasts and a vagina. You are inside yourself, looking at this damned piece of rag on the wall that you are supposed to make a world out of. . . . Inside yourself you are looking at this terrifying unknown and trying to feel, to pull everything you can out of all your experience, to make something. I think a woman or a man creating feel very much the same way.   — GRACE HARTIGAN
1922–

I think it would be reasonable for critics to look upon the art scene and ask themselves 'What are women thinking about the world?' . . . If men seriously said, 'What are women? How are they responding to life as shown in the art?' it would be so interesting!   — ISABEL BISHOP
1902–

I feel totally female. I didn't compete with men and I don't want to look like a man! I love being a lady and dressing up and masquerading and wearing all the fineries. I'm breaking down the idea that the artist has to look poor, with berets.
                   — LOUISE NEVELSON
1900–1988

Historically, women have either been excluded from the process of creating the definitions of what is considered art or allowed to participate only if we accept and work within existing mainstream designations.   — JUDY CHICAGO
1939–

ISTORY & TIME

Art is exalted above religion and race. Not a single solitary soul these days believes in the religions of the Assyrians, the Egyptians and the Greeks. . . . Only their art, whenever it was beautiful, stands proud and exalted, rising above all time.

— EMIL NOLDE
1867–1956

To be able to translate the customs, ideas and appearance of my time as I see them—in a word, to create a living art—this has been my aim.

— GUSTAVE COURBET
1819–1877

Observe that it is a great error to believe that all mediums of art are not closely tied to their time.

— CAMILLE PISSARRO
1830–1903

To me there is no past or future in art. If a work of art does not live in the present, it must not be considered at all.

— PABLO PICASSO
1881–1973

. . . images can shatter the old order leaving nothing the same as before.

— FRANCIS BACON
1909–1992

The visible currents of time hold dangerous shoals. Contemporary estimates are always risky.

— JEAN TINGUELY
1925–

Fine works of art never age, because they are marked by genuine feeling. The language of the passions, the impulses of the heart, are always the same.
— EUGÈNE DELACROIX
1798–1863

Man has not changed, the critical thing for me in relation to the fact of the twentieth century is that essential human qualities of life have remained the same, physically and psychologically. . . . The continuum of human life—that is what makes art sublime.
— LEONARD BASKIN
1922–

I cherish the past while wanting the most out of the present. If I am afraid of anything today, it's of going back to the place where I was before. In isolation. I come from a background of optimists. I do not cultivate loss. I connect. That is the basis of my life.
— MIRIAM SHAPIRO
1923–

I think that only time tells about painting. No artist knows in his own lifetime whether what he does will be the slightest good, because I think it takes at least seventy-five to a hundred years before the thing begins to sort itself out.
— FRANCIS BACON
1909–1992

Every work of art is the child of its time; often it is the mother of our emotions. . . . Efforts to revive the art principles of the past at best produce works of art that resemble a stillborn child.
— WASSILY KANDINSKY
1866–1944

I t is only possible to speak in the language and in the spirit of one's time.
— EUGÈNE DELACROIX
1798–1863

Ancient art was the tyrant of Egypt, the mistress of Greece and the servant of Rome.
— HENRY FUSELI
1741–1825

Listen! There was never an artistic period. There was never an art-loving nation.
— JAMES ABBOT MCNEILL WHISTLER
1834–1903

In the last analysis, the artist may shout from all the rooftops that he is a genius; he will have to wait for the verdict of the spectator in order that his declarations take a social value and that, finally, posterity includes him in the primers of Art History.
—MARCEL DUCHAMP
1887–1968

HUMAN ANATOMY

To draw the human figure it is necessary to know as much as possible about its structure and its movements, its bones and muscles . . .
— THOMAS EAKINS
1844–1916

But above all, the best thing is to draw men and women from the nude and thus fix in the memory by constant exercise the muscles of the torso, back, legs, arms and knees, with bones underneath. Then one may be sure that through much study attitudes in any position can be drawn by help of the imagination without one's having the living form in view.
— GIORGIO VASARI
1511–1574

Study anatomy as a science: then follow the practices that reflect the science. Be methodical and do not quit one part until it is perfectly engraved on your memory.
— LEONARDO DA VINCI
1452–1519

. . . when painting living creatures, first sketch in bones. . . . Then add the sinews and the muscles, finally clothe the bones and muscles with flesh and skin.
— LEON BATTISTA ALBERTI
1404–1472

HUMAN ANATOMY

Do not give to all of the muscles of the figure an exaggerated volume, because, even if they occupy a well defined place, they do not protrude in so prominent a way, unless the member to which they belong is in a study of great force or extreme fatigue. If you proceed otherwise, you will succeed only in representing a sack of nuts and not a human figure.

— LEONARDO DA VINCI
1452–1519

Study muscles so that you know the nature of what you see. . . . Anatomy is a tool like good brushes.   — ROBERT HENRI
1865–1929

I have always tried to express the inner feelings by the mobility of the muscles . . . pass over useless details and seize only upon the truth of the whole.   — AUGUSTE RODIN
1840–1917

I have bought myself a very beautiful book on anatomy. . . . It was in fact very expensive, but it will be of use to me all my life. . . . The key to many things is in thorough knowledge of the human body.   — VINCENT VAN GOGH
1853–1890

Anatomy, that dreadful science! If I had had to learn anatomy, I would never have made myself a painter.

— JEAN-AUGUSTE-DOMINIQUE INGRES
1780–1867

See also The Figure, The Model, and The Nude

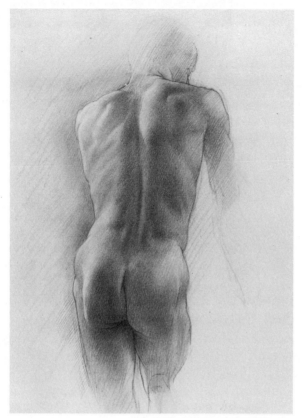

Male Back ▪ *Martha Mayer Erlebacher*
Pencil on paper, 11.9" x 8.9", courtesy of the Arkansas Arts Center Foundation Collection.
Donation Box Acquisition Fund, 1982.

You can spend 20 years in front of the figure and gradually develop a style and a way of dealing with the figure, but that will make you a slave of what's in front of you. But if you study anatomy, then you're freer to make the figure move in space in a way that is different from using the figure as a still-life object.
— MARTHA MAYER ERLEBACHER
1948–

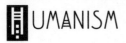UMANISM

I don't like abstract art. I feel that it doesn't really talk about human life in a way that most people can relate to. . . . I was brought up believing that the real content of art is ideas, but it has to be made manifest through some kind of humanistic subject matter.

— MARTHA MAYER ERLEBACHER
1948–

I assume that most people are interested in the hopes, fears, dreams and tragedies of other people.　　— BEN SHAHN
1898–1969

I have always believed, and still believe, that artists who live and work with spiritual values cannot and should not remain indifferent to a conflict in which the highest values of humanity and civilization are at stake.

— PABLO PICASSO
1881–1973

I see myself as standing very much in battle against a whole lot of others who have found a way of working which for me denies the central essence of art, its humanity and its humanness. Their art doesn't tell us about the deepest and most profound ideas of human beings in contact with other human beings.　　　　　　— LEONARD BASKIN
1922–

For thousands of years art was seen as a source of responsible moral and ethical leadership. Today, taking that stance is almost seen as comic.

— JACK BEAL
1931–

Let us try and see, even though we ourselves may not succeed, if we cannot lay the foundations of an art dedicated to mankind. A style of art that will fire man's imagination. An art that springs from our very hearts.

— EDVARD MUNCH
1863–1944

I have tried to emphasize that those people, eating their potatoes in the lamplight, have dug the earth with those very hands they put in the dish. It speaks of manual labor, and how they have honestly earned their food.

— VINCENT VAN GOGH
1853–1890

Any product or activity designed to communicate feelings and ideas—and artworks certainly belong to that category—performs a social function and is therefore implicitly, if not explicitly, also of political import.

— HANS HAACKE
1936–

I feel issues of sex and gender have always been at the core of art, along with all of the other profound concerns of human beings (to name a few—procreation, growth, aggression, hunger, aging, fear, death, etc.). Art is the greatest possible rationalization of our deepest fears, joys, and instincts as human beings.

— MARTHA MAYER ERLEBACHER
1948–

'm convinced that, in the end, art isn't for the artists but for their fellow men.

— GEORGE RICKEY
1907–

After all, art in our society was never natural as, say, in African society. That's why those things that they did were so great. It comes from the fabric of society.

— ALICE NEEL
1900–1984

I would like my pictures to look as if a human being had passed between them, like a snail, leaving a trail of the human presence and memory of the past events as the snail leaves its slime. — FRANCIS BACON
1909–1992

The forging of works of art is one of man's remaining semblances of divinity. Man has been incapable of love, wanting in charity and despairing of hope. He has not molded a life of abundance and peace, and he has charted the earth and befouled the heavens more wantonly than ever before. He has made of Arden a landscape of death. In this garden I dwell, and in limning the horror, the degradation and filth, I hold the cracked mirror up to man. All previous art makes this course inevitable.
— LEONARD BASKIN
1922–

I have tried to express the terrible passions of humanity by red and green.
— VINCENT VAN GOGH
1853–1890

I am content that my art should have purposes outside itself. I would like to exert influence in these times when human beings are so perplexed and in need of help . . . my course is clear and unequivocal.
— KÄTHE KOLLWITZ
1867–1945

We have a fear of mud and blood. But if we are to be anything, if we artists are to survive this period at all—we will survive as spokesmen, never again as entertainers.
— RICO LEBRUN
1900–1964

HUMANISM

Make a drawing flow, stopping sometimes, and going on. Yours should be the drawing of the human spirit through the human form.

— ROBERT HENRI
1865–1929

I should reproach myself if I did not try to make pictures which will arouse serious thoughts.

— VINCENT VAN GOGH
1853–1890

Although the art of all races and of all times has a common value—human, universal—each new cycle must work for itself, must create, must yield its own production—its individual share to the common good.

— JOSÉ CLEMENTE OROZCO
1883–1949

See also Politics

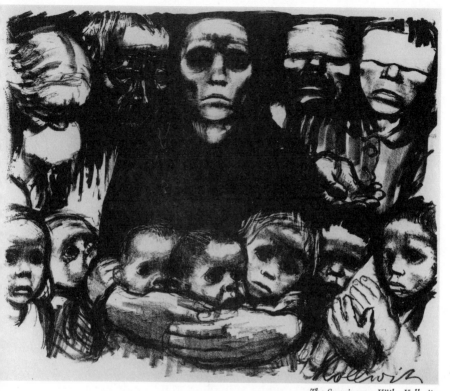

The Survivors ▪ *Käthe Kollwitz*
Lithograph on thin wove paper, 23" x 27.4", 1923, courtesy of the Vivian and Gordon
Gilkey Graphic Arts Collection, Portland Art Museum, Portland, Oregon. G7536.

*While I drew, and wept along with the terrified children I
was drawing, I really felt the burden I am bearing. I felt
that I have no right to withdraw from the reponsibility of
being an advocate. It is my duty to voice the suffering of
men, the neverending sufferings heaped mountain-high.*

— KÄTHE KOLLWITZ
1867–1945

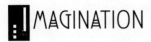

IMAGINATION

United with reason, imagination is the Mother of the Arts and a source of their wonders.

— FRANCISCO DE GOYA
1746–1828

A picture is first of all a product of the imagination of the artist; it must never be a copy. . . . The air we see in the painting of the old masters is never the air we breathe.

— EDGAR DEGAS
1834–1917

Art is the opposite of nature. A work of art can come only from the interior of man.

— EDVARD MUNCH
1863–1944

Logic, where you ponder and, oh dear, it sounds so fancy— what in the hell do you need it for? It measures you and limits you. See now take a word like imagination. Imagination is not vague. Imagination is flash thinking, instantaneous.

— LOUISE NEVELSON
1900–1988

It is the imagination that gives depth and space to a picture.

— HENRI MATISSE
1869–1954

Imagination makes you see all sorts of things.
— GEORGIA O'KEEFFE
1887–1986

A man paints with his brains and not with his hands.
— MICHELANGELO BUONARROTI
1475–1564

The senses deform, the mind forms. Work to perfect the mind. There is no certitude but in what the mind conceives.
— GEORGES BRAQUE
1882–1963

Whether it be Masaccio, Giotto, Greco, Cézanne or Picasso, each had to 'fashion' the natural appearance of objects and their forms, and give them a quality of an imaginary world.
— OSSIP ZADKINE
1890–1967

What is now proven was once only imagined.
— WILLIAM BLAKE
1757–1827

IMAGINATION

What use is my mind? Granted that it enables me to hail a bus and to pay my fare. But once I am inside my studio, what use is my mind? I have my model, my pencil, my paints. My mind doesn't interest me.
— EDGAR DEGAS
1834–1917

The big element is trust, not knowing where you're going, and it will be grander than your imagination. If you know where you are going then it can only be as good as your imagination.
— GEORGE GREEN
1943–

Being an artist means that you have the ability to imagine yourself into all kinds of othernesses. Doing that, you can rearrange perspectives on things, which can provide a revelation.
— ERIC FISCHL
1948–

No amount of skillful invention can replace the essential element of imagination.
— EDWARD HOPPER
1882–1967

You have to have an idea of what you are going to do, but it
should be a vague idea. — PABLO PICASSO
1881–1973

Only an individual can imagine, invent, or create. The whole
audience of art is an audience of individuals.

— BEN SHAHN
1898–1969

*The universe is real but you can't see it.
You have to imagine it. Once you
imagine it, you can be realistic about
reproducing it.*

— ALEXANDER CALDER
1898–1976

I don't know anybody who doesn't have a fantasy. Everybody
must have a fantasy.

— ANDY WARHOL
1927?–1987

See also Creativity and Inspiration

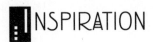NSPIRATION

And suddenly for the first time I saw a painting. . . . it became entirely clear to me that art in general is much more powerful than I had realized and that, on the other hand, painting can develop just as much power as music possesses.

— WASSILY KANDINSKY
1866–1944

I think that when one is young it is the object, the outside world that fires one's enthusiasm; one is carried away by it. In later life, it's something within himself, the need to express an emotion, that leads a painter to choose his point of departure, one form rather than another.

— PIERRE BONNARD
1867–1947

I really do feel that my parents just made it possible for me to be here, but my real ancestors are artists of the past. I'm comforted and excited and soothed and inspired by them. I saw two Vermeers last year that were like having some kind of out-of-body experience. But I could say the same thing for many Poussins and Cézannes.

— JIM DINE
1935–

I have two or three days of some real dismal dragging around hoping that something will get together and strike a spark.

— RICHARD DIEBENKORN
1922–1993

Is it not emotion, the sincerity of one's feelings for nature, that draws us, and if the emotions are sometimes so strong that one works without knowing one works . . . then one must remember that it has not always been so, and that in the time to come there will again be heavy days, empty of inspiration.

— VINCENT VAN GOGH
1853–1890

I go to my studio every day. Some days the work comes easily. Other days nothing happens. Yet on the good days the inspiration is only an accumulation of all the other days, the nonproductive ones.

— BEVERLY PEPPER
1924–

Imitation is not inspiration, and inspiration only can give birth to a work of art. The least of man's original emanations is better than the best of a borrowed thought.

— ALBERT PINKHAM RYDER
1847–1917

Somewhere in the course of their career, artists must learn not merely to despise everything which is not entirely theirs, but must rid themselves completely of this blind fanaticism which drives us to imitate the great masters and swear only by their works. . . . One must learn to be grateful for one's own findings: a handful of naive inspiration is better than anything else.

— EUGÈNE DELACROIX
1798–1863

Inspiration comes to me unexpectedly, never by virtue of deliberate stimulation, never by sitting in a chair: it always happens in front of the easel. — WILLIAM BAZIOTES
1912–1963

Inspiration is indispensable to my work, but it is hard to come by. It is there or it is not—it is a gift of the gods.
— LOUISE BOURGEOIS
1911–

What moves men of genius, or rather what inspires their work, is not new ideas but their obsession with the idea that what has already been said is still not enough.
— EUGÈNE DELACROIX
1798–1863

Only that art is viable which finds its elements in the surrounding environment. As our ancestors drew the matter of their art from the religious atmosphere weighing upon their souls, so we must draw inspiration from the tangible miracles of contemporary life. — UMBERTO BOCCIONI
1882–1916

One must detect and capture the artifices of the great masters, but shrug off all restraint in front of nature and represent it solely by one's own inspiration. — EDGAR DEGAS
1834–1917

Very often I am sitting at dinner and I take out my notebook. I get very inspired when I eat, for some reason.

— CLAES OLDENBURG
1929–

More of me comes out when I improvise.

— EDWARD HOPPER
1882–1967

The artist has only to remain true to his dream and it will possess his work in such a manner that it will resemble the work of no other man. — ALBERT PINKHAM RYDER
1847–1917

It's never a problem figuring out what to do next. What you discover in one painting compels you to do the next.

— GEORGE GREEN
1943–

Guess how I made that head of a bull. One day, in a rubbish heap, I found an old bicycle seat, lying beside a rusted handlebar . . . and my mind instantly linked them together. The idea for this Tête de Taureau came to me before I had even realized it. I just soldered them together. . . .

— PABLO PICASSO
1881–1973

Others may see that art is emotion, inspiration. Those are only phrases with which to amuse the ignorant.

— AUGUSTE RODIN
1840–1917

See also Creativity, Imagination, and Spontaneity and the Subconscious

JOY, PLAY, & PLEASURE

For art and joy go together, with bold openness, and high head, and ready hand—fearing nought, and dreading no exposure.
— JAMES ABBOT MCNEILL WHISTLER
1834–1903

Ultimately, my hope is to amaze myself. The anticipation of discovering new possibilities becomes my greatest joy.
— JERRY UELSMANN
1934–

I offer you pure joy. Look at my sculpture until you manage to see them. Those who are close to God have seen them.
— CONSTANTIN BRANCUSI
1876–1957

Then I drew and painted all through grammar school. For me, the high point of the day was when the paints came out.
— RICHARD DIEBENKORN
1922–1993

Every child is an artist. The problem is how to remain an artist once he grows up.
— PABLO PICASSO
1881–1973

I want to make things that are fun to look at, that have no propaganda value whatsoever.

— ALEXANDER CALDER
1898–1976

The relationship of art and play: play is art—consequently I play furiously. . . . Art is nonsense and—like everything—not senseless.

— JEAN TINGUELY
1925–

I don't believe a state of playfulness necessarily yields better pictures.

— DAVID SALLE
1952–

It is, of course, a luxury to create art and on top of this, to insist on expressing one's own artistic opinion. Nothing is more luxurious than this.

— MAX BECKMANN
1884–1950

All the sorrows, all the bitterness, all the sadnesses, I forget them and ignore them in the joy of working.

— CAMILLE PISSARRO
1830–1903

JOY, PLAY, & PLEASURE

The minute I sat in front of a canvas, I was happy. Because it was a world, and I could do as I like in it. — ALICE NEEL
1900–1984

I was much happier when I had much less responsibility . . . when my only responsibility was to my work and to myself.
— ROBERT RAUSCHENBERG
1925–

For me, 'happiness' has always had a banal sound, like 'inspiration.' Both 'happiness' and 'inspiration' are the words of amateurs.
— DIEGO RIVERA
1886–1957

> *It's true, of course, humor is very important in my life, as you know. That's the only reason for living, in fact.*
> — MARCEL DUCHAMP
> *1887–1968*

When I was a little kid I always drew on the walls, on books, on scrap paper. I loved to draw. It was something to rejoice upon. It was magical. — NANCY GROSSMAN
1940–

I can't understand how anyone is able to paint without optimism. Despite the general pessimistic attitude in the world today, I am nothing but an optimist.
— HANS HOFMANN
1880–1966

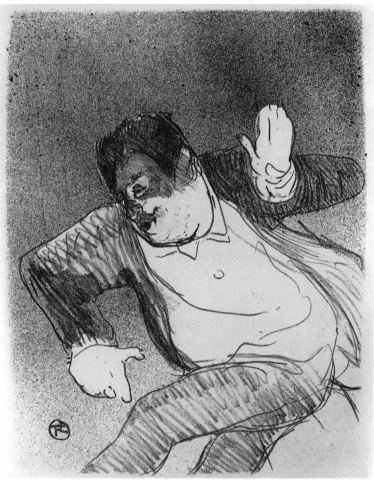

Caudieux Dancing at the Little Casino ▪ *Henri de Toulouse-Lautrec*
Litho print, 10.6" x 8.3", courtesy of the Metropolitan Museum of Art, New York.

*Of course one should not drink much,
but often.*

— HENRI DE TOULOUSE-LAUTREC
1864–1901

The first merit of a picture is to be a feast for the eyes.
— EUGÈNE DELACROIX
1798–1863

*C*hild! You have to be a child to think that
an artist is something useful.
— PAUL GAUGUIN
1848–1903

As for myself, my aim has always been to paint or draw that
which gives me pleasure, the principle being that if an artist is
not happy with his work then others will not be happy with it
either.
— PIERRE ALECHINSKY
1927–

Pretend you are dancing or singing a picture. A worker or painter
should enjoy his work, else the observer will not enjoy it.
— ROBERT HENRI
1865–1929

For me, making art always has something of play about it. I do
hundreds of different things—sketchbooks, drawings on
birchbark, drawings on leaves, even on mushrooms.
— MARY FRANK
1933–

Hardly any of the names of ancient artists are recorded, even
though they did more for the happiness of their people than
the pharaohs, generals and world rulers whose pride filled the
world with sorrow.
— EMILE NOLDE
1867–1956

LANDSCAPE

In showing objects on a landscape, barely indicate the more remote ones, and as they come closer, make them more distinct. . . . Objects close to the observer must show firm color.

— LEONARDO DA VINCI
1452–1519

I bring the landscape home with me.

— HANS HOFMANN
1880–1966

I carry my landscape around with me.

— JOAN MITCHELL
1926–

. . . the landscape was in my arms as I worked.

— HELEN FRANKENTHALER
1928–

I've had people say, why paint American landscapes? . . . If you want something profound, the American countryside is exactly the place.

— ANDREW WYETH
1917–

Therefore, the works I do are a mixture of ideal situation in shape and spontaneity reacting to landscape and a feeling of evoking how I feel, myself bodily, in relation to this landscape.

— DAME BARBARA HEPWORTH
1903–1975

LANDSCAPE

Begin by determining your composition. Then the values—the relation of the forms to the values. These are the basics. Then the color, and finally the finish.

— JEAN-BAPTIST-CAMILLE COROT
1796–1875
on painting a landscape

Painting is a science and should be pursued as an inquiry into the laws of nature. Why, then, may not a landscape be considered as a branch of natural philosophy, of which pictures are but experiments?

— JOHN CONSTABLE
1776–1837

It's enough to drive you crazy, trying to depict the weather, the atmosphere, the ambience.

— CLAUDE MONET
1840–1926

See also Nature

THE LANGUAGE OF ART

Art is a language of symbols.

— PABLO PICASSO
1881–1973

Painting is, in my opinion, a richer language than that of words. . . . Painting is a language much more immediate, and, at the time, much more charged with meaning.

— JEAN DUBUFFET
1901–1985

One could not express in words what one feels with one's eyes and one's hand.

— ALBERTO GIACOMETTI
1901–1966

I found I could say things with color and shapes that I couldn't say in any other way—things that I had no words for.

— GEORGIA O'KEEFFE
1887–1986

Art is a technique of communication. The image is the most complete technique of all communication.

— CLAES OLDENBURG
1929–

I think photography, like most art, is in a weak position as communication. There's not a common syntax—we can't all agree what a rock, a tree or other element in an image might mean. It's much more open ended. But there is a kind of power, an evocative statement that is made that may be focused at a level that is beyond verbalization.

— JERRY UELSMANN
1934–

A painting, for me, speaks by itself: what good does it do, after all, to impart explanations? A painter has only one language.

— PABLO PICASSO
1881–1973

Art is a wholly physical language whose words are all the visible objects.

— GUSTAVE COURBET
1819–1877

Great art is art that strips you of words, and then allows you to find the new words to describe that experience.

— ERIC FISCHL
1948–

See also Communication

LIGHT & SHADOW

Shadow is the absence of light, merely the obstruction of the luminous rays by an opaque body. Shadow is of the nature of darkness. Light (on an object) is of the nature of luminous body; one conceals and the other reveals.

— LEONARDO DA VINCI
1452–1519

I certainly agree that abundance and variety of color contribute greatly to the charm and beauty of a picture. But I would have artists be convinced that the supreme skill and art in painting consists in knowing how to use black and white. And every effort and diligence is to be employed in learning the correct use of these two pigments because it is light and shade that make objects appear in relief. And so black and white give solidity to painted things.

— LEON BATTISTA ALBERTI
1404–1472

If I could have had my own way, I would have confined myself to black and white.

— EDGAR DEGAS
1834–1917

Each movement changes as well the way the form's revealed by light: the shadows, reflection and local color are in constant flux.

— PHILIP PEARLSTEIN
1924–

You see these thick curtains shut out the daylight: artificial light suits me a great deal better; it's absolutely steady, and much more exciting.

— PABLO PICASSO
1881–1973

What is beautiful is not always well and good. I submit the thought to painters who are so attached to the beauty of colors that they hate to put the least shadow on them, giving not a thought to the beautiful relief given to figures by a proper gradation and strength of shadow.

— LEONARDO DA VINCI
1452–1519

The first two things to study are form and values. For me, these are the basis of what is serious in art.

— JEAN-BAPTIST-CAMILLE COROT
1796–1875

Look closely at the Japanese; they draw admirably and yet in them you will see life outdoors and in the sun without shadows. . . . I will move as far away as possible from whatever gives the illusion of a thing, and as shadow is the trompe l'oeil of the sun, I am inclined to do away with it.

— PAUL GAUGUIN
1848–1903

. . . who always talks about line, never about masses. But where does one see lines in nature? I see only masses in light and masses in shadow, planes that come forward and planes into recession.

— FRANCISCO DE GOYA
1746–1828

In spite of the absence of shadows or halftones expressed by hatchings, I do not renounce the play of values or modulations. I modulate with variations in the weight of the line, and all with areas it delimits on the white paper. I modify different parts of the white paper without touching them, but by their relationships.

— HENRI MATISSE
1869–1954

The first of all simple colors is white, although some would not admit that either black or white are colors, the first being a source or a receiver of colors, and the latter totally deprived of them. But you can't leave them out: since painting is but an effect of light and shade, that is chiaroscuro.

— LEONARDO DA VINCI
1452–1519

The illusion of three-dimensional forms in space grows out of my attempt to re-create the fall of light over the actual forms in front of me.

— PHILIP PEARLSTEIN
1924–

> *The first goal of a painter is to be able to make a simple flat surface appear like a relief . . . this is done by the correct use of light and shade. The one who can do this deserves the most praise.*
>
> — LEONARDO DA VINCI
> *1452–1519*

Work a great deal with evening effects, a lamp, a candle, etc. The tantalizing thing is not always to show the source of light, but the effects of light.

— EDGAR DEGAS
1834–1917

[Light] . . . the soul and medium of art.

— JOHN CONSTABLE
1776–1837

The only light that really exists [is] that in the artist's brain.

— HENRI MATISSE
1869–1954

INE

Draw lines, young man, many lines, from memory or from nature—it is in this way that you will become a good artist.

— JEAN-AUGUSTE-DOMINIQUE INGRES
1780–1867
advice given to Degas

The line has in itself neither matter nor substance and may rather be called an imaginary idea, rather than a real object.

— LEONARDO DA VINCI
1452–1519

One must always search for the desire of the line, where it wishes to enter or where to die away.

— HENRI MATISSE
1869–1954

The grip of a line. Note how a line takes hold. It hooks the vital parts together. It binds the composition.

— ROBERT HENRI
1865–1929

Everyone knows that even a single line may convey an emotion.

— PIET MONDRIAN
1872–1944

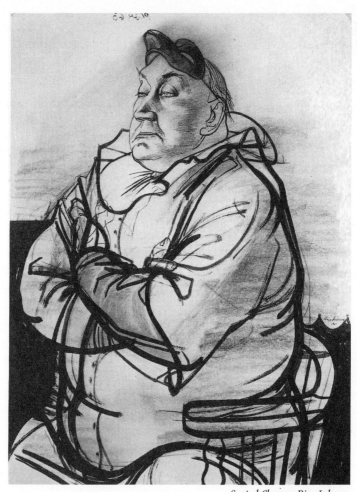

Seated Clown ▪ *Rico Lebrun*
Ink and wash, red and black chalk, 30" x 40", 1941, courtesy of the
Santa Barbara Museum of Art, California. Gift of Mr. and Mrs. Arthur B. Sachs.

True lines do not exist in nature; we
invent them. They are poetic fiction.
— RICO LEBRUN
1900–1964

THE MODEL

Only the mature artist who works from a model is capable of seeing the body for itself, only he has the opportunity for prolonged viewing.

— PHILIP PEARLSTEIN
1924–

Whenever I wait for a model, every time, even when I am the most pressed for time, I am overjoyed when the hour passes and I tremble when I hear the key turn in the door.

— EUGÈNE DELACROIX
1798–1863

In front of the model I work with the same will to reproduce truth as if I were making a portrait. I do not correct nature, I incorporate myself into it; it directs me. I can only work with a model. The sight of human forms nourishes and comforts me.

— AUGUSTE RODIN
1840–1917

No single man can be taken as a model for a perfect figure, for no man lives on earth who is endowed with the whole of beauty.

— ALBRECHT DÜRER
1471–1528

I work from the people that interest me, and that I care about, in rooms that I live in and know. I use the people to invent my pictures, and I can work more freely when they are there.

— LUCIAN FREUD
1922–

THE MODEL

[My models are like] living landscapes arranged like still lifes in
my studio.   — PHILIP PEARLSTEIN
1924–

My models, my human figures, are never like extras in an
interior. They are the main theme of my work. I depend
absolutely on my model. . . . The emotional interest which they
inspire in me is not particularly visible in the representation of
their bodies, but often in certain lines and special values which
are spread throughout the canvas or paper and which form its
orchestration, its architecture. . . . The model for me is a
touchstone, it is a door which I must break open in order to
reach the garden in which I am alone and feel good, even the
model exists only for what use I can make of it.
                                                    — HENRI MATISSE
1869–1954

It is good for young people to have a model, but they should
forego looking at the model while they paint.
                                                    — PAUL GAUGUIN
1848–1903

The first thing to attend to in painting the model are the
movements and the general color. The figure must balance,
appear solid and of the right weight. The movement, once
understood, every detail of the action, will be an integral part
of the main continuous action; every detail of color auxiliary to
the main system of light and shade.
                                                    — THOMAS EAKINS
1844–1916

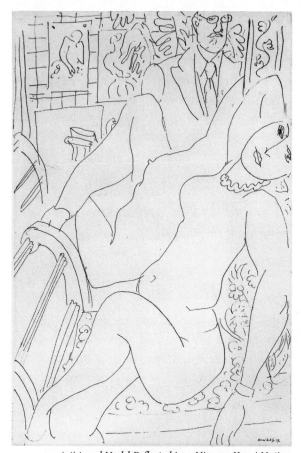

Artist and Model Reflected in a Mirror ▪ *Henri Matisse*
Pen and ink on paper, 24.8" x 16", 1937, courtesy of the Baltimore Museum of Art.
The Cone Collection, formed by Dr. Claribel Cone and Miss Etta Cone
of Baltimore, Maryland. BMA 1950.12.51.

*The living model, the naked body of a woman, is the privileged seat
of feeling, but also of questioning. . . . The model must mark you,
awaken in you an emotion which you seek in turn to express.*

— HENRI MATISSE
1869–1954

Very few life-studies are strong enough to live. If you work from memory, you are most likely to put in your own feeling.

— ROBERT HENRI
1865–1929

The only ones who can really benefit by consulting the model are those who can produce their effect without a model.

— EUGÈNE DELACROIX
1798–1863

Michelangelo . . . has made his figures stand out so marvelously. For this work he first made models in clay or wax, and from these, because they remain stationary, he took the outlines, the lights, and the shadows, rather than from the living model.

— GIORGIO VASARI
1511–1574

The professional model is always like a stuffed owl. These girls are alive.

— HENRI DE TOULOUSE-LAUTREC
1864–1901
referring to the girls of the bordellos

See also The Figure, Human Anatomy, and The Nude

MYSTICISM, MAGIC, & SPIRITUALITY

Something sacred, that's it. It's a word that we should be able to use, but people would take it in the wrong way. You ought to be able to say a painting is as it is, with its capacity to move us, because it is as though it were touched by God.

— PABLO PICASSO
1881–1973

The job of the artist is always to deepen the mystery.

— FRANCIS BACON
1909–1992

The painting is not on a surface, but on a plane which is imagined. It moves in a mind. It is not there physically at all. It is an illusion, a piece of magic, so what you see is not what you see.

— PHILIP GUSTON
1913–1980

The merit of a painting is undefinable . . . in a word, it is what the spirit adds to color and line that appeals to the soul.

— EUGÈNE DELACROIX
1798–1863

A work of art is finished, from the point of view of the artist, when feeling and perception have resulted in a spiritual synthesis.

— HANS HOFMANN
1880–1966

Let us not delude ourselves by the seemingly scientific nature of the darkroom ritual; it has been and always will be a form of alchemy.
— JERRY UELSMANN
1934–

There are some things in painting which cannot be explained, and that something is essential.
— PIERRE AUGUSTE RENOIR
1841–1919

To transform three into two dimensions is for me an experience full of magic in which I glimpse for a moment that fourth dimension which my whole being is seeking.
— MAX BECKMANN
1884–1950

> *P*ainting isn't an aesthetic operation; it's *a form of magic designed as a mediator between this strange, hostile world and us, a way of seizing the power by giving form to our terrors as well as our desires.*
> — PABLO PICASSO
> *1881–1973*

The magic of painting is when you turn a canvas on its edge, and it is only one-sixteenth of an inch thick on an old piece of linen. I'm excited by all that illusion and color that comes from just moving minerals mixed with oil around on a surface. In this age of technology, there are still more digits in a Chinese bristle brush and human brain than there are in a computer.
— JAMES ROSENQUIST
1933–

I paint not by sight but by faith. Faith gives you sight.

— AMOS FERGUSON

I myself do nothing. The Holy Spirit accomplishes all things through me.

— WILLIAM BLAKE
1757–1827

I would like to express man's relation to the world and to himself—and to some spiritual force outside himself.

— GEORGE TOOKER
1920–

The mystical will always be with us. . . . A whole mass of things that cannot be rationalized—new born thoughts that are still not properly formed.

— EDVARD MUNCH
1863–1944

At one time the earth was supposed to be flat . . . yet the probability is that life, too, is spherical and much more extensive and capacious than the hemisphere we know.

— VINCENT VAN GOGH
1853–1890

Art seems to me to be above all a state of soul. All souls are sacred, the soul of all the bipeds in every quarter of the globe.

— MARC CHAGALL
1889–1985

Religion is everywhere. It is in the mind, in the heart, in the love you put into what you do.

— PIERRE AUGUSTE RENOIR
1841–1919

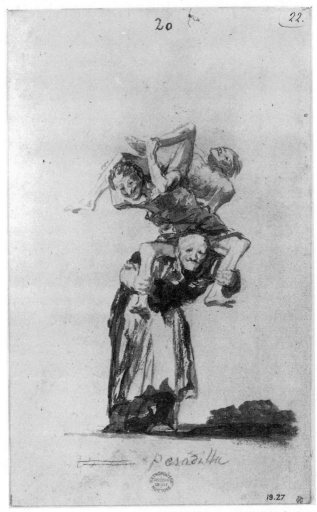

The Nightmare ▪ *Francisco de Goya*
Brush and wash, black ink on white paper, 9.2" x 15.7", courtesy of the
Metropolitan Museum of Art, New York. Rogers Fund, 1919. All rights reserved.

The dream of Reason produces monsters.

— FRANCISCO DE GOYA
1746–1828

You look at my pictures . . . there's witchcraft and hidden meaning there.
— ANDREW WYETH
1917–

When spiritual, metaphysical, material, or immaterial events come into my life, I can only fix them by way of painting.
— MAX BECKMANN
1884–1950

Take me, I am the drug; take me, I am hallucinogenic.
— SALVADOR DALI
1904–1989

Everything has two aspects: the current aspect, which we see nearly always and which ordinary men see, and the ghostly and metaphysical aspect, which only rare individuals may see in moments of clairvoyance and metaphysical abstraction.
— GIORGIO DE CHIRICO
1888–1978

The true work of art is but a shadow of the divine perfection.
— MICHELANGELO BUONARROTI
1475–1564

God is really another artist, like me.
— PABLO PICASSO
1881–1973

They tell you that a tree is only a combination of chemical elements. I prefer to believe that God created it, and that it is inhabited by a nymph.
— PIERRE AUGUSTE RENOIR
1841–1919

ATURE

The observation of nature is part of an artist's life.
— HENRY MOORE
1898–1986

And nature is just as varied and just as beautiful in our day as she was in the time of Phidias.
— THOMAS EAKINS
1844–1916

Nature is so much richer than anything you can imagine.
— GEORGE TOOKER
1920–

To achieve progress nature alone counts, and the eye is trained through contact with her.
— PAUL CÉZANNE
1839–1906

Keep your love of nature, for that is the true way to learn to understand art more and more.
— VINCENT VAN GOGH
1853–1890

There is no recipe for improving nature. The only thing is to see.
— AUGUSTE RODIN
1840–1917

If the painter works directly from nature, he ultimately looks for nothing but momentary effects; he does not compose, and soon he gets monotonous.
— PIERRE AUGUSTE RENOIR
1841–1919

Even in front of nature, one must compose. — EDGAR DEGAS
1834–1917

To work from nature is to improvise. — GEORGES BRAQUE
1882–1963

I prefer every time a picture composed and painted
outdoors. . . . This making studies and then taking them home
to use them is only half right. You get the composition, but you
lose the freshness. . . . — WINSLOW HOMER
1836–1910

Creation on the part of great artists is only their particular way
of seeing, coordinating and rendering nature.
— EUGÈNE DELACROIX
1798–1863

*Nature contains the elements, in color and
form, of all pictures, as the keyboard
contains the notes of all music. But the artist is
born to pick and choose . . . as the musician
gathers his notes, and forms his chords, until
he brings forth from chaos, glorious harmony.*
— JAMES ABBOT MCNEILL WHISTLER
1834–1903

I cannot copy nature in a servile way, I must interpret nature and
submit it to the spirit of the picture. — HENRI MATISSE
1869–1954

NATURE

Salvation lies in nature, now more than ever.
— CAMILLE PISSARRO
1830–1903

Painting from nature is not copying the object, it is realizing one's sensation. — PAUL CÉZANNE
1839–1906

To say to the painter, that nature is to be taken as she is, to say to the player, that he may sit on the piano.
— JAMES ABBOT MCNEILL WHISTLER
1834–1903

I came to the simple solution, through feeling and thinking, that the aims (and thus the means) of nature and art are essentially, organically, and by universal law different from each other—and equally great and equally strong. . . . This solution liberated me and opened up new worlds.
— WASSILY KANDINSKY
1866–1944

Architecture completes nature. It marks an advance of human intellect in the field of metaphysical discoveries.
— GIORGIO DE CHIRICO
1888–1978

The beautiful is in nature, and it is encountered under the most diverse forms of reality. Once it is found it belongs to art, or rather to the artist who discovers it. — GUSTAVE COURBET
1819–1877

Yet in reality, what are the most sublime productions of the pencil but selections of some of the forms of nature, and copies of a few of her evanescent effects; and this is the result, not of inspiration, but of long and patient study, under the direction of much good sense. — JOHN CONSTABLE
1776–1837

Whoever thinks he can remember the infinite teaching of nature flatters himself. Memory is not that huge. — LEONARDO DA VINCI
1452–1519

There is courage indeed in launching a frontal attack upon the main structure and main lines of nature, and cowardice in approaching by facets and details: art is really a battle.
— EDGAR DEGAS
1834–1917

Nature is one thing and painting is quite another. — PABLO PICASSO
1881–1973

To call everything that appears illogical 'fantasy,' fairy tale, or chimera would be practically to admit not understanding nature. — MARC CHAGALL
1889–1985

NATURE

Treat nature in terms of the cylinder, the sphere, the cone, everything in proper perspective. — PAUL CÉZANNE
1839–1906

The artist has been the element of nature, and the arbiter of nature; he who has sat on a cloud and viewed it from afar, but at the same time has identified himself as one of nature's parts. The true artist views nature from his own time.
— DAVID SMITH
1906–1965

There's a quote from Hamlet that is my guide. . . . He tells the players not to exaggerate but to hold a mirror up to nature. Don't overdo it, don't underdo it. Do it just on the line.
— ANDREW WYETH
1917–

The creation of a work of art must of necessity, as a result of entering into the specific dimensions of pictorial art, be accompanied by distortion of the natural form. For, therein is nature reborn. — PAUL KLEE
1879–1940

See also Landscape

THE NUDE

The members of an architectural structure follow the laws exemplified in the human body. He who . . . is not a good master of the nude . . . cannot understand the principles of architecture.

— MICHELANGELO BUONARROTI
1475–1564

Traditionally the Nude was used to express formulations about life as larger-than-life or more-perfect-than-life; as Heroic or Ideal. . . . The nude is not a 'genre' subject.

— ISABEL BISHOP
1902–

Nudity, of course, is a problem for Americans. It disrupts our social exchange.

— ERIC FISCHL
1948–

There is nothing in all the world more beautiful or significant of the laws of the universe than the nude human body. In fact, it is not only among the artists but among all people that a greater appreciation and respect for the human body should develop. When we respect the nude, we will no longer have any shame about it.

— ROBERT HENRI
1865–1929

I think it's the most important study there is and the most challenging and the most difficult.   — WAYNE THIEBAUD
1920–
on drawing the nude

I have unbounded admiration for the nude. I worship it like a god.
— AUGUSTE RODIN
1840–1917

When you draw a nude, sketch the whole figure and nicely fit the members to it and to each other. Even though you may only finish one portion of the drawing, just make certain that all the parts hang together, so that the study will be useful to you in the future.   — LEONARDO DA VINCI
1452–1519

When an artist or student draws a nude figure with painstaking care, the result is drawing, and not emotion.
— HENRI MATISSE
1869–1954

This is the human animal occupied with herself, a cat licking herself. Hitherto the nude has always been represented in poses which presuppose an audience. But my women are simple, honest creatures who are concerned with nothing beyond their physical occupations. Here is another one, washing her feet—it is as if you were looking through a keyhole.

— EDGAR DEGAS
1834–1917

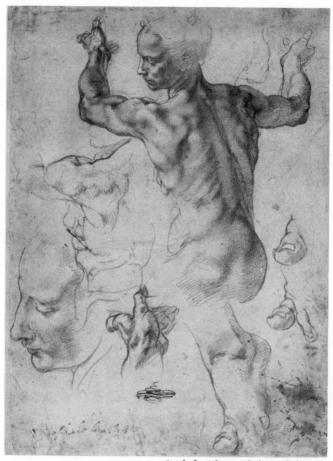

Study for Libyan Sibyl ▪ *Michelangelo*
Red chalk on paper, 11.4" x 8.4", courtesy of the Metropolitan Museum of Art,
New York. Purchase, 1924, Joseph Pulitzer Bequest. All rights reserved.

And who is so barbarous as not to understand that the foot of a man is nobler than his shoe, and his skin nobler than that of the sheep with which he is clothed.

— MICHELANGELO BUONARROTI
1475–1564

A nude by Degas is chaste. But his women wash in tubs! . . .
Just the way it is at home. — PAUL GAUGUIN
1848–1903

The nude, if you tackle it, is a very fascinating subject,
especially for a woman. — ISABEL BISHOP
1902–

The nakedness of woman is the work of God.
— WILLIAM BLAKE
1757–1827

*The nude is exquisite, the most
beautiful thing in the world.*
— ROBERT HENRI
1865–1929

Beautiful nudes made it possible for us to contemplate our
sexuality in safety. — MARTHA MAYER ERLEBACHER
1948–

There is nothing more banal than these statues of recent
notabilities, to be seen in every big city of Europe,
masquerading as tailors' models of their ugly period. Man's
naked form, on the other hand, belongs to no particular
moment in history; it is eternal, and can be looked upon with
joy by the people of all ages.

— AUGUSTE RODIN
1840–1917

See also The Figure, Human Anatomy, and The Model

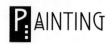

PAINTING

Painting relates to both art and life. Neither can be made. I try to act in the gap between the two.

— ROBERT RAUSCHENBERG
1925–

Painting is a state of being.
— JACKSON POLLOCK
1912–1956

Painting is just another way of keeping a diary.

— PABLO PICASSO
1881–1973

Painting is concerned with the ten things you can see; these are: darkness and brightness, substance and color, form and place, remoteness and nearness, movement and rest.

— LEONARDO DA VINCI
1452–1519

In painting, as in the other arts, there's not a single process, no matter how insignificant, which can be reasonably made into a formula.

— PIERRE AUGUSTE RENOIR
1841–1919

What has reasoning to do with painting?

— WILLIAM BLAKE
1757–1827

. . . liberate painting from the shackles of probability.

— PAUL GAUGUIN
1848–1903

One simply paints—one doesn't paste one's idea on a painting.

— PABLO PICASSO
1881–1973

I was unable to divorce paint, as it was traditionally, from the fact that it was just another material. Paint has a character, a quality, it has a physical, recognizable body and I just couldn't cultivate in myself that other kind of illusionary quality that I would have to have believed in in order to have gone in a different direction. I have the same trouble with canvas—I knew what it was—it's a piece of cloth. And after you recognize that the canvas you're painting on is simply another rag then it doesn't matter whether you use stuffed chickens or electric light bulbs or pure forms.

— ROBERT RAUSCHENBERG
1925–

Painting, like poetry, selects in the universe whatever she deems most appropriate to her ends.

— FRANCISCO DE GOYA
1746–1828

Painting must do for the eyes what poetry does for the ears.
— ANTOINE COZPEL
1661–1722

As music is the poetry of sound, so is painting the poetry of sight, and the subject-matter has nothing to do with harmony of sound or of color.
— JAMES ABBOT MCNEILL WHISTLER
1834–1903

During the process of painting, one draws.
— PAUL CÉZANNE
1839–1906

Painting is drawing, with the additional means of color.
— JOHN SLOAN
1871–1951

The place where I had freedom was when I painted. When I painted I was completely and utterly myself. For that reason it was extremely important to me.
— ALICE NEEL
1900–1984

Painting is self-discovery.
— JACKSON POLLOCK
1912–1956

A painting is never finished—it simply stops in interesting places.
— PAUL GARDNER
20th century

A painted picture is like a vehicle. One can either sit in the driveway and take it apart or one can get in it and go somewhere.

— MARK TANSEY
1949–

The painter who stands before an empty canvas must think in terms of paint.

— BEN SHAHN
1898–1969

I think it takes a long time to work a painting. . . . The more paint you put on, the more alive the surface looks, the more you're defining what you want. It's like, why don't you just do one draft of a short story? Because the content isn't clear, and the content really is the painting.

— JENNIFER BARTLETT
1941–

Painting is an attempt to come to terms with life. There are as many solutions as there are human beings.

— GEORGE TOOKER
1920–

Painting is a very difficult thing. It absorbs the whole man, body and soul—thus I have passed blindly many things which belong to real and political life.

— MAX BECKMANN
1884–1950

A painting is not thought out and fixed before hand, while one is painting it. It follows the mobility of one's thoughts.

— PABLO PICASSO
1881–1973

I have told myself a hundred times that painting—that is to say, the material thing called painting—was no more than the pretext, the bridge between the mind of the painter and that of the spectator.

— EUGÈNE DELACROIX
1798–1863

The painter makes real to others his innermost feelings about all that he cares for. A secret becomes known to everyone who views the picture through the intensity with which it is felt.

— LUCIAN FREUD
1922–

The painting is not on a surface, but on a plane which is imagined. It moves in a mind. It is not there physically at all. It is an illusion, a piece of magic. — PHILIP GUSTON
1913–1980

The act of painting is not a duplication of experience, but the extension of experience on the plane of formal invention.

— STUART DAVIS
1894–1964

PAINTING

*P*ainting is special, separate, a matter of
meditation and contemplation . . .

— AD REINHARDT
1913–1967

Perspective is to painting what the bridle is to the horse, the
rudder to a ship.

— LEONARDO DA VINCI
1452–1519

Painting is self-discovery. You arrive at the image through the
act of painting.

— ADOLPH GOTTLIEB
1903–1974

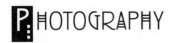PHOTOGRAPHY

Photography has every right and every merit to claim our
attention as the art of our age. — ALEXANDER RODCHENKO
1891–1956

Personally, I am committed to the medium and I make no
apologies for it. I have gradually confused photography with life
and, as the result of this, I believe I am able to work out of myself
at an almost precognitive level. — JERRY UELSMANN
1934–

. . . not through the technique at his command, but through
his vision of the world does the photographer create pictures of
significance and lasting value. — BEAUMONT NEWHALL
20th century

*When you see what you express through
photography, you realize all the things
that can no longer be the objectives of
painting. Why should an artist persist in
treating subjects that can be established so
clearly with the lens of a camera?*
— PABLO PICASSO
1881–1973

One should photograph things not only for what they are but
for what else they are. — MINOR WHITE
1908–1976

PHOTOGRAPHY

Do you know what will soon be the ultimate in truth?—
photography, once it begins to reproduce colors, and that won't
be long in coming. And yet you want an intelligent man to
sweat for months so as to give the illusion he can do something
as well as an ingenious little machine can!

— PAUL GAUGUIN
1848–1903

The camera is objective. . . . I never said the camera was truth.
It is, however, a more accurate and more objective way of
seeing.
— CHUCK CLOSE
1940–

There is one thing the photograph must contain, the humanity
of the moment. This kind of photography is realism. But
realism is not enough—there has to be vision and the two
together can make a good photograph. It is difficult to describe
this thin line where matter ends and mind begins.

— ROBERT FRANK
1924–

I find that I'm beginning to be able to do things that aren't in
the photograph, simply because certain things are in my
repertoire, so to speak. . . . Just the nature of painting
something brings it out sharper, too, because the brush gives a
nice sharp line, and in a photograph it could be a fuzzy line.

— RICHARD ESTES
1932–

My pictures speak only when we both listen.

— BRETT WESTON
1911–

My dearest one, the camera has rendered impotent any attempt to compete with it. This has to be accepted as a necessary and a scientific advance. What reason, therefore, remains to sit in realism's stagnation?

— ARSHILE GORKY
1904–1948

One of the things that I love about photography is that the problems are never entirely resolved. It's always full of surprises; no matter how often you've done something in a certain way, the results are never quite identical. Photography is something that you learn all your life.

— MORLEY BAER
1916–

Each click of the shutter suggests an emotional and visual involvement and contains the potential of establishing greater rapport with some quintessential aspect of the subject and my feelings toward it.

— JERRY UELSMANN
1934–

Sometimes I get to places just when God's ready to have somebody click the shutter.

— ANSEL ADAMS
1902–1984

PHOTOGRAPHY

I would like the synthesized and reconstructed images I create to challenge the inherent believability of the photograph. All the information is there, and yet the mystery remains.

— JERRY UELSMANN
1934–

I do not think any photograph can really be abstract. I prefer the term 'extract' for I cannot change the optical realities, but only manage them in relation to themselves and the format.

— ANSEL ADAMS
1902–1984

Photography has arrived at a point where it's capable of liberating painting from all literature, from the anecdote and even from the subject. . . . So shouldn't painters profit from their newly acquired liberty, and make use of it to do other things?

— PABLO PICASSO
1881–1973

The imitator is a poor kind of creature. If the man who paints only the tree, or flower, or other surface he sees before him were an artist, the king of the artists would be the photographer.

— JAMES ABBOT McNEILL WHISTLER
1834–1903

The camera will never compete with the brush and palette until such time as photography can be taken to Heaven or Hell.

— EDVARD MUNCH
1863–1944

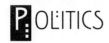

POLITICS

So called political art. . . . The term reduces the works it refers to to a crude, one dimensional reading. Worse, however, it implies that works which are not called 'political' have indeed no ideological and therefore no political implications. This, of course, is a fallacy. — HANS HAACKE
1936–

One can analyze epoch after epoch—from the stone age to our own day—and see that there is no form of art which does not also play an essential political role.

— DIEGO RIVERA
1886–1957

No, painting is not made to decorate apartments. It's an offensive and defensive weapon against the enemy.
— PABLO PICASSO
1881–1973

Everybody knows artists don't change society, but that's too easy a way to put it. Artists are part of the information process. . . . Visual history is important in providing a record of what is going on—levels of intention, levels of confidence, levels of aggression or control.

— LEON GOLUB
1922–

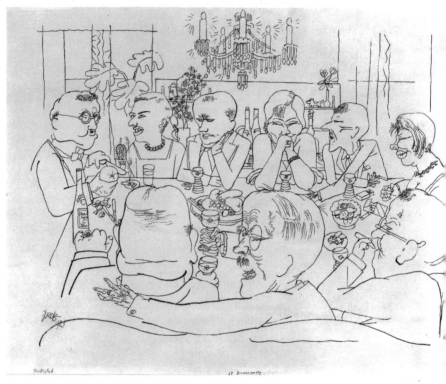

Dinner Party ■ *George Gr...*
Pen and black ink, 16.4" x 21.6", courtesy of the Portland Art Mus...
Portland, Oregon. Ella Hirsch F...

*My drawings and paintings were done as an act of
protest; I was trying by means of my work to convince
the world that it is ugly, sick and hypocritical.*

— GEORGE GROSZ
1893–1959

The state is not competent in artistic matters. . . . When the state leaves us free, it will have carried out its duty.
— GUSTAVE COURBET
1819–1877

The Arts and Sciences are the Destruction of Tyrannies or Bad Governments. Why should A Good Government endeavor to Depress what is its Chief and only support?
— WILLIAM BLAKE
1757–1827

You know, there are many more things in my paintings that are against war than people think. Not just Guernica.
— PABLO PICASSO
1881–1973

Paintings don't change wars. They show feelings about wars.
— LEON GOLUB
1922–

To think that painters once thought that they could paint 'The Massacre of the Innocents.'
— PABLO PICASSO
1881–1973
said upon visiting Auschwitz at the end of World War II

See also Humanism

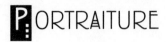

PORTRAITURE

Every time I paint a portrait I lose a friend.

— JOHN SINGER SARGENT
1859–1925

When I painted his portrait and offered it to him, he glanced at the canvas, then, looking at himself in the mirror, thought a moment and said: 'Well, no! Keep it!'

— MARC CHAGALL
1889–1985

I'm very interested in trying to do portraits, which now is almost an impossible thing to do, because you either make an illustration or you make an abstract suggestion. The point is, you never know what stroke will make an illustration or a charged and meaningful appearance.

— FRANCIS BACON
1909–1992

In order for a portrait to be a work of art, it must not resemble the sitter.

— UMBERTO BOCCIONI
1882–1916

Creativity with portraits involves the invocation of a state of rapport when only a camera stands between two people . . . mutual vulnerability and mutual trust.

— MINOR WHITE
1908–1976

I would wish my portraits to be of the people, not like them. Not having a look of the sitter, being them.

— LUCIAN FREUD
1922–

If the artist only reproduces superficial features as photography does, if he copies the lineaments of a face exactly, without reference to character, he deserves no admiration. The resemblance which he ought to obtain is that of the soul.

— AUGUSTE RODIN
1840–1917

Ah! Portraiture, portraiture with the thought, the soul of the model in it, that is what I think must come.

— VINCENT VAN GOGH
1853–1890

Like Chekhov, I am a collector of souls. . . . I think if I hadn't been an artist, I could have been a psychiatrist.

— ALICE NEEL
1900–1984

I think it is important to be autobiographical. What I try to do in my work is explore myself in physical terms—to explain something in terms of my own sensibilities.

— JIM DINE
1935–

I have a voice like a hornet in an oil jar . . .
My eyes are purplish, spotted and dark.
My teeth are like the keys of an instrument,
for by their moving the voice sounds or falls still.
My face has a shape which strikes terror.
My clothes are such as chase crows to the wind . . .
A spider-web lies hidden in my one ear,
while all night long a cricket chirrups in the other.
— MICHELANGELO BUONARROTI
1475–1564
written in his seventies

I remember that at one time I always made a drawing before
going to bed!!—Of myself I mean—though I finally destroyed
most of them. — JAMES ABBOT MCNEILL WHISTLER
1834–1903

I loathe my own face, and I've done self-portraits because I've
had nobody else to do. — FRANCIS BACON
1909–1992

If nature had a fixed model for the proportions of the face,
everyone would look alike and it would be impossible to tell
them apart; but she has varied the pattern in such a way that
although there is an all but invisible standard as to size, one
clearly distinguishes one face from another.
— LEONARDO DA VINCI
1452–1519

*T*he character of a face in a drawing
depends not upon its various proportions,
but upon a spiritual light which it reflects.
— HENRI MATISSE
1869–1954

One doesn't paint what someone looks like, but what effect he has.
— RICHARD LINDNER
1901–1978

There is nothing more intereseting than people. One paints
and one draws to learn to see people, to see oneself.
— PABLO PICASSO
1881–1973

I don't think I'm really a portrait painter, because I only use a
head to express something more. And if a painting stays just a
head, I'm not satisfied with it. If it's an outdoor person, I feel
that his countenance reflects the skies he walks under, the
clouds have reflected on his face for his whole life, and I try to
get that quality into the portrait. — ANDREW WYETH
1917–

Artists deal with gesture. They get to know a great deal about
people. A sitter may not say a word for an hour, but the body
has been speaking all the time. A work of art in itself is a
gesture and it may be warm or cold, inviting or repelling.
— ROBERT HENRI
1865–1929

PORTRAITURE

You know, if one paints someone's portrait, one should not know him if possible. No knowledge! I do not want to know him at all, want to see what is there, the outside. The inner follows by itself. It is mirrored in the visible. — OTTO DIX
1891–1969

And yet this portrait, as close as it is to his real self, is a paraphrase of the greatest mystery and, in the last analysis, it does not represent a single personality but a part of that spirituality or feeling which pervades the whole world.
— ERNST LUDWIG KIRCHNER
1880–1938

Make portraits of people in typical, familiar poses, being sure above all to give their faces the same kind of expression as their bodies.

— EDGAR DEGAS
1834–1917

Our mouths, those public but also intimate apertures, are designed for speaking. But they also swallow, suck, blow, bite, and suffer. They are a means of access to our interior space.
— FRANCIS BACON
1909–1992

For nearly 20 years I have concerned myself exclusively with the portrait. . . . I paint my friends. . . . I am interested in the richness and complexity of the portrait head (the skin, pores, individual hairs, reflections all presented in a high degree of detail) coupled with an equally extreme attitude of economy and simplicity in the working methods.

— CHUCK CLOSE
1940–

I did a portrait of myself for Vincent, who had asked me for one. I think it's one of my best things: thoroughly incomprehensible—it is so abstract! A bandit's head at first glance . . . also personifying an Impressionist painter who is frowned upon and in the eyes of the world always carries a chain.

— PAUL GAUGUIN
1848–1903

One day while I was drawing a young girl something struck me: that is to say, all of a sudden I noticed the only thing that remained alive was the gaze. . . . In a living person there is no doubt that what makes him alive is his gaze. If the gaze, that is to say life itself, becomes essential, there is no doubt that what is essential is the head.

— ALBERTO GIACOMETTI
1901–1966

For me the painting is the person.

— LUCIAN FREUD
1922–

QUALITY & PERFECTION

A good artist ought never to allow impatience to overcome his sense of the main end of art—perfection.

— MICHELANGELO BUONARROTI
1475–1564

That painting is the most praiseworthy which is most like the thing represented. — LEONARDO DA VINCI
1452–1519

My aim in painting has always been the most exact transcription possible of my most intimate impression of nature. If this end is unattainable, so, it can be said, is perfection in any other ideal of painting or in any other of man's activities. — EDWARD HOPPER
1882–1967

To express the same thing, but express it better. It is always necessary to seek perfection.
— PABLO PICASSO
1881–1973

If in your drawing you habitually disregard proportions you become accustomed to the sight of distortion and lose critical ability. — ROBERT HENRI
1865–1929

If my paintings are worth anything—if they have quality—that quality will find a way to preserve itself. — ANDREW WYETH
1917–

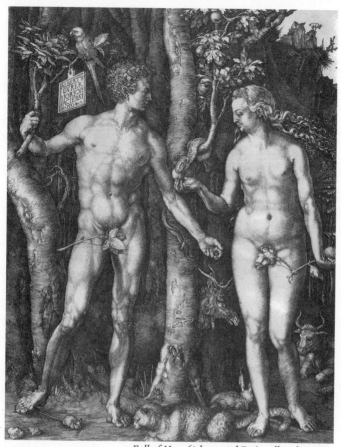

Fall of Man (Adam and Eve) ▪ *Albrecht Dürer*
Engraving, 9.9" x 7.6", 1504, courtesy of the Metropolitan Museum of Art, New York.
Fletcher Fund, 1919. All rights reserved. 19.73.1.

*I hold that the perfection of form and beauty is contained
in the sum of all men. . . . For the human figure must,
once and for all, remain different from those of other
creatures, let them [the painters] fashion them otherwise
just as they please.*
                                                    — ALBRECHT DÜRER
                                                        1471–1528

QUALITY & PERFECTION

I'm always saying to myself: 'That is not right yet. You can do better.' It's rare when I can prevent myself from taking a thing up again. . . . Sometimes it becomes an obsession.

— PABLO PICASSO
1881–1973

One man may sketch something with his pen on half a sheet of paper in one day and it turns out to be better than another's big work at which the author labors with the utmost diligence for a whole year. — ALBRECHT DÜRER
1471–1528

Artists who seek perfection in everything are those who cannot attain it in anything.

— EUGÈNE DELACROIX
1798–1863

A picture is finished when all trace of the means used to bring about the end has disappeared.

— JAMES ABBOTT MCNEILL WHISTLER
1834–1903

And I would even venture to affirm that a man cannot attain excellence if he satisfies the ignorant and not those of his own craft. — MICHELANGELO BUONORROTI
1475–1564

If you worry about how good the art is, you're never going to make your own art. — ERIC FISCHL
1948–

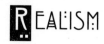EALISM

Realism is by essence the art of democracy.

— GUSTAVE COURBET
1819–1877

People who have developed a commitment to realism have a stronger and deeper commitment to all the aspects of art than people who are working in other genres. Because it so much absorbs you, so much involves you, that you cannot do it half-heartedly.

— JACK BEAL
1931–

I'm bothered by being called a realist painter. . . . I think that all painting is abstract. The best figurative painting is abstract. I mean, the whole idea of painting is abstract.

— WILLIAM BAILEY
1930–

The fact that I see nature in abstract terms perhaps means that the aesthetics of abstraction wins the struggle for my aesthetic soul, but in the course of my pursuit I have learned to look at what is in front of me without idealization. . . .

— PHILIP PEARLSTEIN
1924–

The distance between any work of art and the immediate reality of no matter what has become too great, and in fact only reality interests me now and I know I could spend the rest of my life in copying a chair.

— ALBERTO GIACOMETTI
1901–1966

REALISM

I have such a strong romantic fantasy about things—and that's what I paint, but come to it though realism. If you don't back up your dreams with truth, you have a very round-shouldered art.

— ANDREW WYETH
1917–

Art is more than mere chronicle. It must mirror the intellect and the emotion, for anyone, even a commerical artist or illustrator, can portray realism.

— ARSHILE GORKY
1904–1948

Art should create an experience. This is hard to do in abstractions. But it's what makes representation relevant and dramatic for me.

— ERIC FISCHL
1948–

Greatness in art is the free, significant and profound expression of reality. And by reality is meant the penetration beneath surfaces to the true meaning of things in their relationship to life.

— LEONARD BASKIN
1922–

I've tried to make images that would unlock the values of feeling on different levels. For me, to be as realistic as possible has meant extreme deformations.

— FRANCIS BACON
1909–1992

For me reality remains exactly as virginal and unexplored as the first time anyone tried to represent it.

— ALBERTO GIACOMETTI
1901–1966

I always aim at the resemblance. An artist should observe nature but never confuse it with painting. It is only translatable into painting by signs.

— PABLO PICASSO
1881–1973

What is most real for me are the illusions I create with my paintings.

— EUGÈNE DELACROIX
1798–1863

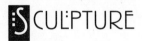CULPTURE

What is the meaning of sculpture? Today when we are all
conscious of the expanding universe, the forms experienced by
sculpture should express not only this consciousness but
should, I feel, emphasize also the possibilities of new
developments of the human spirit, so that it can affirm and
continue life in its highest form. The story is still the same as
that of the Gothic or any other culture. . . . Sculpture
communicates an immediate sense of life—you can feel the
pulse of it. . . . In sculpture we have a complete orientation of
body and mind.

— DAME BARBARA HEPWORTH
1903–1975

I am a sculptor because the shape of things matters more to me
than the colour of them. . . . For me, it is the three-
dimensional reality and shape which one wants to understand,
to grasp and to experience. This is, I think, what makes me a
sculptor. . . . I want to produce the complete thing, rather than
a sketch or an illusion of it.

— HENRY MOORE
1898–1986

If you ask me why I make sculpture, I must answer that it is
my way of life, my balance, and my justification for being. If
you ask me for whom do I make art, I will say that it is for all
who approach it without prejudice.

— DAVID SMITH
1906–1965

You do not make sculpture because you like wood. That is absurd. You make sculpture because the wood allows you to express something that another material does not allow you to.
— LOUISE BOURGEOIS
1911–

Carving is a source of joy to the artist. . . . To attack the raw material, gradually to extract a shape out of it following one's own desire, or, sometimes, the inspiration of the material itself: this gives the sculptor great joy. In carving, material and thought are linked by the hand alone; thus the raw material is imbued with a warmth of feeling directly drawn from the artist's nature.
— ARISTIDE MAILLOL
1861–1944

What produces good sculpture is a good mind.
— HENRY MOORE
1898–1986

. . . sculpture could be just a deepening impression, like a fossil . . . also drawing in charcoal or ink [could be] sculptures risen to the surface, colors flaking off—swept and raked off. A gardening of the paper.
— MARY FRANK
1933–

SCULPTURE

Gravitation is the only logical factor a sculptor has to contend with. The parts can't float, as in painting, but must be tied together.

— DAVID SMITH
1906–1965

Sculpture is quite simply the art of depression and protuberance.

— AUGUSTE RODIN
1840–1917

Sculpture, by its nature, is a thing. The sculptor is dealing with space itself, rather than the illusion of space.

— GEORGE RICKEY
1907–

You can't make a sculpture, in my opinion, without involving your body. You move and you feel and you breathe and you touch. . . . Touch, and poise, wind and water, everything. Sculpture is involved in the body living in the spirit or the spirit living in the body, whichever way you like to put it.

— DAME BARBARA HEPWORTH
1903–1975

I like to be called a sculptor and I feel that a feminine mind certainly can move in any direction.

— LOUISE NEVELSON
1900–1988

No, when I begin a sculpture I invent, I am simply very attentive and I am taken by images. . . . What is essential when you work is not to lose the image you have. It's like a dream come to the light of day. You have to hold fast to it, not let it escape.

— GIACOMO MANZÚ
1908–

Detail does not interest me; what matters is the general idea. . . . I seek architecture and volume. . . . Sculpture is architecture, the equilibrium of masses, a composition of taste. . . . I always start with a geometric figure, a cube, a lozenge, a triangle, because these figures hold their position in space best of all.

— ARISTIDE MAILLOL
1861–1944

You see, I think a sculptor has to be a practical person. He can't be just a dreamer . . . you must be a workman; you must be somebody with his feet on the ground.

— HENRY MOORE
1898–1986

Clay is an alive material so you have to put tremendous restraint on it, not allow the fingers to become involved in tiny formulations, keep it big and broad and strong.

— LEONARD BASKIN
1922–

SCULPTURE

A great deal of sculpture since Brancusi has been a matter of concentrating on the expressive possibilities of the material one uses. This, I think, will always be a very important part of painting and sculpture. . . . But I do feel very strongly that this is only a part of the question—that it's a great mistake to think that art begins and ends with a sensitive response to material. All the very great periods of art have been, in fact, conceptual in origin. The beginning of art is a feeling—is an idea—is a concept—is a state of mind, and one uses material to manifest something which corresponds to that and I wouldn't like to think that the sculpture I make is a mere exploration of the material I use.

— REG BUTLER
1913–1981

And what is this volume? It is the space that an object occupies in the atmosphere. The essential basis of art is to determine that exact space; this is the alpha and omega, this is the general law. . . . For instance to make a bust does not consist in executing the different surfaces and their details. . . . On the contrary, from the first sitting the whole mass must be conceived and constructed in its varying circumferences. . . . Each profile is actually the outer evidence of the interior mass; each is the perceptible surface of a deep section.

— AUGUSTE RODIN
1840–1917

I began to do sculpture because that was precisely the realm in which I understood least. I couldn't endure having it elude me completely. I had no choice.

— ALBERTO GIACOMETTI
1901–1966

I so love carving. It seems to me to be the most rhythmic and marvelous way of working on live and sensuous material. . . . Every piece of wood and every piece of stone has its own particular live quality of growth, crystal structure, and one becomes utterly absorbed and blended rhythmically within the cutting of this. — DAME BARBARA HEPWORTH
1903–1975

To most people who look at a mobile, it's no more than a series of flat objects that move. To a few, though, it may be poetry.
— ALEXANDER CALDER
1898–1976

To achieve poetry in a piece of sculpture, one must know how to dream, how to draw the dreams, and how to see the interwebbed, interdependent dance of this beautifully colored energy field that we too bluntly call 'life' or 'world.'
— MARK DISUVERO
1933–

SCULPTURE

For my taste sculpture should have as little movement as possible.
— ARISTIDE MAILLOL
1861–1944

Possibly steel is so beautiful because of all the movement
associated with it, its strength and functions. . . . Yet it is also
brutal; the rapist, the murderer and death-dealing giants are
also its offspring.
— DAVID SMITH
1906–1965

I'm interested in making things that are as machinelike as possible.
— GEORGE RICKEY
1907–

. . . there was the possibility of pure mechanism, of the
chromatics of movement. And that became a purely sculptural
thing. Today I don't even make a distinction between the
machine and sculpture.
— JEAN TINGUELY
1925–

*No painter ought to think less of sculpture
than of painting and no sculptor less of
painting than of sculpture.*
— MICHELANGELO BUONARROTI
1475–1564

SEEING & PERCEIVING

Art, to me, is seeing. I think you have got to use your eyes as well as your emotions, and one without the other just doesn't work.

— ANDREW WYETH
1917–

A fool sees not the same tree that a wise man sees.

— WILLIAM BLAKE
1757–1827

*It is not enough to believe what you see,
you must also understand what you see.*

— LEONARDO DA VINCI
1452–1519

And with painting, you have to educate yourself as a viewer by seeing more and more. The more you see, the more you understand.

— JENNIFER BARTLETT
1941–

. . . man learns while he sees and what he learns influences what he sees.

— EDWARD HALL
19th century

Actually you see things differently all the time depending on the light, the nature of the day, the way your eyes are focused, the mood you are in. Your focus keeps changing. Your head is always moving. All these things are happening and it is all changing your perception.
— JANET FISH
1938–

It is necessary to keep one's compass in one's eyes and not in the hand, for the hands execute, but the eye judges.
— MICHELANGELO BUONARROTI
1475–1564

I grant you that the artist does not see Nature as she appears to the vulgar, because his emotions reveal to him the hidden truths beneath appearances . . . his eye grafted on his heart reads deeply into the bosom of Nature. That is why the artist has only to trust his eyes.
— AUGUSTE RODIN
1840–1917

You do not see with the lens of the eye. You see through that, and by means of that, but you see with the soul of the eye.
— JOHN RUSKIN
1819–1900

The artist does not draw what he sees, but what he must make others see.
— EDGAR DEGAS
1834–1917

I shut my eyes in order to see.

— PAUL GAUGUIN
1848–1903

What I hear is valueless; only what I see is living, and when I close my eyes my vision is even more powerful.

— GIORGIO DE CHIRICO
1888–1978

*Art does not reproduce what we see.
It makes us see.*

— PAUL KLEE
1879–1940

I do not paint what I see—but what I saw.

— EDVARD MUNCH
1863–1944

I paint things not as I perceive them but as I conceive them.

— PABLO PICASSO
1881–1973

My work is about seeing—seeing things like they haven't been seen before.

— ROBERT MAPPLETHORPE
1946–1989

Sometimes I see it and then paint it. Other times I paint it and then see it.

— JASPER JOHNS
1930–

Nobody sees a flower—really—it is so small it takes time—we haven't time—and to see takes time, like to have a friend takes time.
— GEORGIA O'KEEFFE
1887–1986

I am interested in the idea of sight, in the use of the eye. I am interested in how we see and why we see the way we do.
— JASPER JOHNS
1930–

Try to reduce everything you see to the utmost simplicity. That is, let nothing but the things which are of the utmost importance to you have any place . . . there are lots of clever people who can paint 'anything,' but lacking the seeing power, paint nothing worth while. . . . Seeing is not such an easy thing as it is supposed to be.
— ROBERT HENRI
1865–1929

These works are about my eyes. I've tried to teach them to be ruthless and kind.
— JIM DINE
1935–

Sight is the noblest sense of man.
— ALBRECHT DÜRER
1471–1528

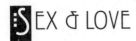# Sex & Love

Love and sex can go together and sex and unlove can go together and love and unsex can go together. But personal love and personal sex is bad.

— ANDY WARHOL
1927?–1987

Every picture shows a spot with which the artist himself has fallen in love.

— ALFRED SISLEY
1839–1899

Painting is like making love. You cannot ask, 'How do you do it?' But, hopefully, it is beautiful.

— FRANCESCO CLEMENTE
1952–

I think one's art goes as far and as deep as one's love goes.

— ANDREW WYETH
1917–

Whores are the most honest girls, they present the bill right away. The others hang on and never let you go. When one lives with problems of importance, the prostitute is ideal. You pay, and whether or not you fail is of no importance. She doesn't care.

— ALBERTO GIACOMETTI
1901–1966

Painting and fucking a lot are not compatible; it weakens the brain.
— VINCENT VAN GOGH
1853–1890

Well, I suppose sex really is the greatest act of aggression in the world. But women want it. . . . It is aggression, but it's the law of life. But they don't have to accept other insults.
— ALICE NEEL
1900–1984

Was it because she took my first kiss, that she took away my life's breath. Was it that she lied—she deceived—that one day suddenly the scales fell from my eyes and I saw a Medusa's head and I saw life as a thing of terror.
— EDWARD MUNCH
1863–1944

I feel sorry for men who are always running after women. What a job! On duty day and night: not a minute's respite. I've known painters who never did any good work because instead of painting their models they seduced them.
— PIERRE AUGUSTE RENOIR
1841–1919

But it's true, isn't it Pauline, that people imagine that the artists and their models spend their time getting up to all sorts of obscenities? As far as work goes, well, they paint or sculpt when they are tired of enjoying themselves. . . .

— EDGAR DEGAS
1834–1917

*T*hose who restrain desire, do so because
theirs is weak enough to be restrained.

— WILLIAM BLAKE
1757–1827

Sex is more exciting on the screen and between the pages than between the sheets.

— ANDY WARHOL
1927?–1987

Marriage! What a calamity in our day!

— PAUL GAUGUIN
1848–1903

I have a wife too many already, namely this art, which harries me incessantly, and my works are my children.

— MICHELANGELO BUONARROTI
1475–1564

Embraces are cominglings from the head even to the feet, and not a pompous high priest entering by a secret place.

— WILLIAM BLAKE
1757–1827

Art isn't something you marry. It's something you rape.

— EDGAR DEGAS
1834–1917

The function of muscle is to pull and not to push, except in the case of the genitals and the tongue.

— LEONARDO DA VINCI
1425–1519

In love, there's sentiment and passion; I know only sentiment through myself, passion through others. I hear certain voices I know say: sentiment=love of the intellect; I can answer: passion=the love of the body.

— BERTHE MORISOT
1841–1895

You cannot simplify love by cutting away all but its essence.

— RICO LEBRUN
1900–1964

The paintings that really excite me have an erotic element or side to them irrespective of subject matter.

— LUCIAN FREUD
1922–

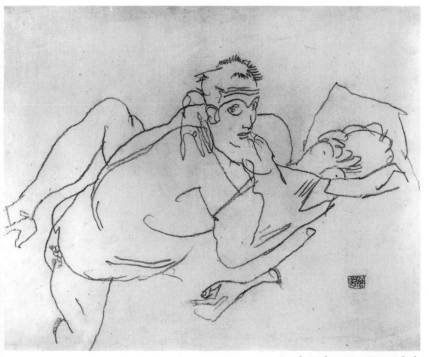

Couple Embracing ▪ *Egon Schiele*
Black oil crayon on paper, 16.1" x 20.4", 1916, courtesy of the
Santa Barbara Museum of Art. Anonymous gift to the Ala Story Collection.

*I do not deny that I have made drawings and watercolors
of an erotic nature. But they are always works of art. Are
there no artists who have done erotic pictures? . . . I shall
not try to find excuses. That would be beneath me.*

— EGON SCHIELE
1890–1918

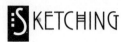

SKETCHING

Out of the artist's impetuous mood they are hastily thrown off, with pen or other drawing instrument or with charcoal, only to test the spirit of that which occurs to him, and for this reason we call them sketches.

— GIORGIO VASARI
1511–1574

There is a great appetite to work, and then my sketchbook serves me as a cookbook when I am hungry. I open it and the least of my sketches can offer me material for work.

— GEORGES BRAQUE
1882–1963

The original idea, the sketch, which is so to speak the egg or embryo of the idea. . . . Just the thing that makes of this sketch the essential expression of the idea is not the suppression of details, but their complete subordination to the big lines which are, before all else, to create the impression.

— EUGÈNE DELACROIX
1798–1863

Have you ever noticed that when recopying a sketch, done in a moment of emotion, and with which you are content, only an inferior copy results, especially if you correct the proportions, the mistakes your reason tells you are there?

— PAUL GAUGUIN
1848–1903

It always helps me to work from the facts of nature. The innumerable sketches I've made contribute to my memories.
— EDWARD HOPPER
1882–1967

Sketch quickly with light strokes on your pad (which you should always have with you), and when it is full, start another, never rubbing out but keeping all carefully, because the forms and motions of the bodies are so infinitely various that they cannot possibly be retained in the memory. Therefore preserve your sketches, for they are your assistants and your masters.
— LEONARDO DA VINCI
1452–1519

To prepare one's work is first to nourish one's feelings by studies which have a certain analogy with the picture, and it is through this that the choice of elements can be made. It is these studies which permit the painter to free his unconscious mind.
— HENRI MATISSE
1869–1954

See also Drawing and Line

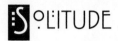OLITUDE

A painter should be a solitary. Solitude is essential to his art. Alone you belong to yourself only; with even one other person you are only half yourself, and you will be less and less yourself in proportion to the number of companions.

— LEONARDO DA VINCI
1452–1519

A very young painter is seldom alone. If he is an art student, he is in an art school with other students. He does not as yet know that one day he will have to face himself as a solitary creature enclosed in a space of four walls . . . and that he will have to be a self-propelled being, with no one at his side.

— PIERRE ALECHINSKY
1927–

Because I cannot work except in solitude, it is necessary that I live my work and that is impossible except in solitude.

— PABLO PICASSO
1881–1973

Often whole days pass without my speaking to anyone.

— VINCENT VAN GOGH
1853–1890

But what I like above all is serenity.

— PIERRE AUGUSTE RENOIR
1841–1919

Artists having lost their savagery, and no longer able to rely upon instinct, one might better say imagination . . . and now they cannot work except in disorderly crowds. . . . This is why it is useless to advise solitude for everyone; one must be strong enough to endure it and to work alone.

— PAUL GAUGUIN
1848–1903

I frequently lock myself in my studio. I do not often see the people I love, and in the end I shall suffer for it . . . painting is one's private life.

— EDGAR DEGAS
1834–1917

You see, it takes me forever to do a painting, and for that you need peace and quiet. . . . — CATHERINE MURPHY
1946–

With Jackson there was quiet solitude. Just to sit and look at the landscape. An inner quietness. After dinner, to sit on the back porch and look at the light. No need for talking. For any kind of communication. — LEE KRASNER
1908–1983
on Jackson Pollock

SOLITUDE

What interests me most about the act of painting is that it is a
solitary act. . . . Of course, when one is faced with a canvas,
one is no longer alone, and the sense of solitude diminishes.
This can be an agreeable passage of time. In fact, solitude then
becomes a kind of companion.   — PIERRE ALECHINSKY
1927–

The painter or draftsman ought to be solitary, in order that the
well-being of the body may not sap the vigor of the mind.
— LEONARDO DA VINCI
1452–1519

It seems to me that today, if the artist wishes to be serious—to
cut out a little original niche for himself, or at least to preserve
his own innocence of personality—he must once more sink
himself in solitude.   — EDGAR DEGAS
1834–1917

You talk of the emptiness you feel everywhere; it is just that
very thing that I feel myself.   — VINCENT VAN GOGH
1853–1890

I work alone (I haven't ever found a way of working other than
in considerable privacy), and I go to quite considerable lengths
to insure that. . . . I don't find it possible to lose myself in the
activity if there are other people around.   — REG BUTLER
1913–1981

Neither Imperial Russia, nor the Russia of the Soviets needs
me. They don't understand me. I am a stranger to them. I'm
certain Rembrandt loves me.   — MARC CHAGALL
1889–1985

I was talking to Brice Marden the other day, and I told him he'd better get used to loneliness. Actually, I don't really think that's sad. I just think it comes from some kind of mysterious drive that almost eliminates all other things that are, of course, a lot more fun. — ROBERT RAUSCHENBERG
1925–

It becomes always more painful for me to finish my work. The older I grow, the more I find myself alone.
— ALBERTO GIACOMETTI
1901–1966

If you're a painter, you're not alone. There's no way to be alone.
— FRANZ KLINE
1910–1962

Everywhere in the modern world there is neglect, the need to be recognized, which is not satisfied. Art is a way of recognizing oneself, which is why it will always be modern.
— LOUISE BOURGEOIS
1911–

I realized also that the artist is always alone. Early in life I had thought I needed other people to confirm or approve what I was doing. . . . It was important for me to learn that what I wanted was really no different from what other artists wanted: confidence that I could be my own censor, my own audience, my own competition. — BEVERLY PEPPER
1924–

SPONTANEITY & THE SUBCONSCIOUS

The painting has a life of its own. I try to let it come through.

— JACKSON POLLOCK
1912–1956

In the brush doing what it's doing, it will stumble on what one couldn't do by oneself.

— ROBERT MOTHERWELL
1915–1991

I believe in an unconscious. So it's possible to say that something causes something and you're not aware of it. You just do what you do.

— JASPER JOHNS
1930–

One never knows what one is going to do. One starts a painting and then it becomes something quite different.

— PABLO PICASSO
1881–1973

Only when he no longer knows what he is doing does the painter do good things.

— EDGAR DEGAS
1834–1917

You are lost the instant you know what the result will be.

— JUAN GRIS
1887–1927

If I think, everything is lost.

— PAUL CÉZANNE
1839–1906

To become truly immortal, a work of art must escape all human limits: logic and common sense will only interfere. But once those barriers are broken, it will enter the realms of childhood visions and dreams.

— GIORGIO DE CHIRICO
1888–1978

In painting, execution should always be extempore. Execution will be beautiful only on condition that the painter lets himself go a little, discovers as he paints.

— EUGÈNE DELACROIX
1798–1863

I would like to write the way I do my paintings, that is, as fantasy takes me, as the moon dictates, and come up with a title long afterward.

— PAUL GAUGUIN
1848–1903

I know that in my own work the best things are the things that just happened—images that were suddenly caught and that I hadn't anticipated. . . . I believe in a deeply ordered chaos and in the rules of chance.

— FRANCIS BACON
1909–1992

With me, it's much more a matter of just accepting whatever happens, accepting all these elements from the outside and then trying to work with them in a sort of free collaboration. That's what makes painting an adventure, which is what it is for me.
— ROBERT RAUSCHENBERG
1925–

It is the seduction which determines the choice of motif and corresponds exactly to the final painting. If this seduction, this initial conception vanishes, all that remains is the motif.
— PIERRE BONNARD
1867–1947

What I want to show in my work is the idea which hides itself behind so-called reality. I am seeking for the bridge which leads from the visible to the invisible. . . . My aim is always to get hold of the magic of reality and to transfer this reality into paint.
— MAX BECKMANN
1884–1950

The mind loves the unknown. It loves images whose meaning is unknown, since the meaning of the mind itself is unknown.
— RENÉ MAGRITTE
1898–1967

I'll take weeks out doing drawings, watercolor studies, I may never use. I'll throw them in a backroom, never look at them again or drop them on the floor and walk over them. But I feel that the communion that has seeped into the subconscious will eventually come out in the final picture.

— ANDREW WYETH
1917–

So far as visual artists are concerned, I think that they are able to work with the material from their subconscious mind without control. . . . That is to say, that the information is permitted to flow through without blockage, and the reason why some people are not able to produce a visual art is, in my opinion, due to the fact that their conscious mind acts as a barrier, and they are only able to produce work which is controlled entirely by their conscious mind without a free association.

— LYNN CHADWICK
1914–

And here in my isolation I can grow stronger. Poetry seems to come of itself, without effort, and I need only let myself dream a little while painting to suggest it.

— PAUL GAUGUIN
1848–1903

I paint as I feel like painting. . . . An artist has to be spontaneous.

— ÉDOUARD MANET
1832–1883

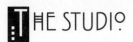HE STUDIO

The artist needs but a roof, a crust of bread, and his easel, and all the rest God gives him in abundance.

— ALBERT PINKHAM RYDER
1847–1917

The windows of your studio should look north so that the light will remain constant throughout the day.

— LEONARDO DA VINCI
1452–1519

My own workshop is a small factory with the same make and quality tools used by production factories.

— DAVID SMITH
1906–1965

Artist's studios do not look like galleries, and when an artist's studio does, everyone is suspicious.

— ALLEN KAPROW
1927–

In the studio all distinctions disappear. One has neither name nor family; one is no longer the daughter of one's mother, one is oneself and individual, and one has before one art, and nothing else. One feels so happy, so free, so proud!

— MARIE BASHKIRTSEFF
1860–1884

I feel most real to myself in the studio.

— ROBERT MOTHERWELL
1915–1991

Before my friends entered the studio, they always had to wait. That was nice to give me time to tidy up, to put on my clothes, for I worked in the nude. In general, I can't stand clothes, I'd rather not wear them and I have no taste in dressing.

— MARC CHAGALL
1889–1985

It is my conviction that the darkroom is capable of being, in the truest sense, a visual research lab; a place for discovery, observation, and meditation.

— JERRY UELSMANN
1934–

The artist should not sacrifice his ideals to a landlord and a costly studio. A rain-tight roof, frugal living, a box of colors, and God's sunlight through clear windows keep the soul attuned and the body vigorous for one's daily work.

— ALBERT PINKHAM RYDER
1847–1917

I may not be there in the studio but I am there in my mind. I am sustaining it until I get to work tomorrow morning. I can't be thinking about other things or writing letters or doing anything else. I am carrying this painting. I am pregnant with it. I can't drop it. I have to carry it through because it is about halfway there. It's all-consuming.

— GRACE HARTIGAN
1922–

STYLES

A lofty style, grave and decorous, [is] essential to great work.
— MICHELANGELO BUONARROTI
1475–1564

The duty of the artist is to strain against the bonds of the existing style.
— PHILIP JOHNSON
1900–1964

. . . no true artist ends with the style that he expected to have when he began, any more than anyone's life unrolls in the particular manner that one expected when young . . . it is only by giving oneself up completely to the painting medium that one finds oneself and one's own style. . . .
— ROBERT MOTHERWELL
1915–1991

And it began to dawn on me that all these men were very stubbornly looking at the world their own way and that fancy word style *had to do with a strong-minded guy deciding this is how he wanted to look at the world.*
— GEORGE SEGAL
1924–

Art does not expand, it repeats itself.
— EDGAR DEGAS
1834–1917

Different motives inevitably require different methods of expression.

— PABLO PICASSO
1881–1973

Abstract is not a style. I simply want to make a surface work. . . . Style in painting has to do with labels.

— JOAN MITCHELL
1926–

The distinction fine art versus other art is extremely important. . . . Sometimes artists take an anti-art attitude simply because they're reacting against the pressure of an art establishment or an art mannerism or an art manner or fashion that becomes oppressive.

— AD REINHARDT
1913–1967

The most striking quality common to all primitive art is its intense vitality. It is something made by people with a direct and immediate response to life.

— HENRY MOORE
1898–1986

There can be no schools; there are only painters.

— GUSTAVE COURBET
1819–1877

I believe in 'let all the flowers bloom'—once a tenet of Mao Tse Tung. I do not believe any movement should monopolize the market.
— ALICE NEEL
1900–1984

Basically I am perhaps a painter without style. Style is often something which locks the painter into the same vision, the same technique, the same formula during years and years, something during one's whole lifetime. . . . I'm never fixed and that's why I have no style.
— PABLO PICASSO
1881–1973

You will say, those schools are merely formal trappings. . . . I compared these formal trappings, with the Pope of Rome, sumptuously garbed, to the naked Christ, or the ornate church, to prayer in the open fields.
— MARC CHAGALL
1889–1985

I'd rather see figures in chariots flying off the tops of our buildings than cubes and rectangles in parks.
— ERIC FISCHL
1948–

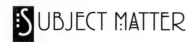UBJECT MATTER

The subject is to a painter what the rails are to a locomotive.
He cannot do without it. — DIEGO RIVERA
1886–1957

There is always a subject; it's a joke to suppress the subject, it's
impossible. — PABLO PICASSO
1881–1973

The main subject is the surface, which has its own laws, over
and above those of the objects. — PIERRE BONNARD
1867–1947

*Oh, young artist, you search for a
subject—everything is a subject, your
subject is yourself, your impressions, your
emotions in the presence of nature.*
— EUGÈNE DELACROIX
1798–1863

. . . anything containing the spark of humanity, containing the
spirit of the age, is interesting. — ÉDOUARD MANET
1832–1883

SUBJECT MATTER

If you let everything go, you are left only with yourself, and that is not enough. One must always have a subject, no matter how insignificant, in order to keep a foot on the ground.

— PIERRE BONNARD
1867–1947

I ndeed, whatever exists in the universe, whether in essence, in act, or in the imagination, the painter has first in his mind and then in his hands.

— LEONARDO DA VINCI
1452–1517

All paintings start out of a mood, out of a relationship with things or people, out of a complete visual impression . . . a painter is bound to reflect himself and his times.

— RICHARD DIEBENKORN
1922–1993

The thing is to describe the object we have gotten to know, with a depth of penetration achieved through feeling.

— ANDREW WYETH
1917–

The day is coming when a single carrot freshly observed will set off a revolution.

— PAUL CÉZANNE
1839–1906

I see drawing and pictures in the poorest huts, in the dirtiest
corner. — VINCENT VAN GOGH
1853–1890

The commonplace is the thing, but it's hard to find. Then if
you believe in it, have a love for it, this specific thing will
become a universal. — ANDREW WYETH
1917–

One loves and gives art only to the things to which one is
accustomed. New things capture your fancy and bore you by
turns. — EDGAR DEGAS
1834–1917

If Chardin, for instance, painted onions and peaches, it's
because he painted in the country, near his kitchen.
— PABLO PICASSO
1881–1973

*If one does not want to paint a still-life or a
landscape or a figure now, one can paint an
Albers or a Rothko or a Kline. . . . Western art is
built on the biographical passion of one artist for
another. . . . Any artist, however, who looks only
into his own life for ideas is still going to find the
irresistible ideas of other artists there.*
— ELAINE DE KOONING
1920–

SUBJECT MATTER

There isn't a person, a landscape, or a subject that doesn't possess at least some interest—although sometimes more or less hidden. When a painter discovers this hidden treasure, other people immediately exclaim at its beauty.

— PIERRE AUGUSTE RENOIR
1841–1919

I borrow some subject or other from life or from nature, and using it as a pretext, I arrange lines and colors so as to obtain symphonies, harmonies that do not represent a thing that is real.

— PAUL GAUGUIN
1848–1903

A painter can turn pennies into gold, for all subjects are capable of being transformed into poems.

— JEAN-AUGUSTE-DOMINIQUE INGRES
1780–1867

There should be no more paintings of interiors, of people reading and women knitting. In the future, they should be people who breathe, who feel emotions, who suffer and live.

— EDVARD MUNCH
1863–1944

Symbolism can be limiting and dangerous. But I don't care for art without it.

— GEORGE TOOKER
1920–

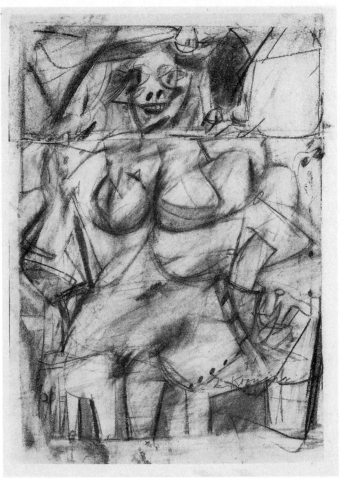

Standing Woman ▪ *Willem de Kooning*
Pastel and pencil on cut and pasted paper, 12" x 9.5", courtesy of the
Museum of Modern Art, New York. The Lauder Foundation Fund.

*Women irritate me sometimes. I painted that
irritation in the 'Woman' series. That's all.*

— WILLEM DE KOONING
1904–1997

SUBJECT MATTER

I don't even want my images of people, clothed or unclothed,
to have meaning other than to be representations of models in
my studio. As a rose is a rose, so my paintings of models are
paintings of models. — PHILIP PEARLSTEIN
1924–

Artists (fine ones) don't copy nature, and when they do record
quite literally the presentation is such as to arouse connotations
quite apart from the subject matter.

— EDWARD WESTON
1886–1958

*After all, the error rests in the mistaken
idea that the subject of a painting is the
object painted.*

— ROBERT HENRI
1865–1929

. . . today painters do not have to go to a subject matter outside
of themselves. Most modern painters work from a different
source. They work from within. — JACKSON POLLOCK
1912–1956

Making a painting about the idea of making a painting is an
idea that appeals to me. — GEORGE GREEN
1943–

When I use objects, I see them as a vocabulary of feelings. I can spend a lot of time with objects, and they leave me as satisfied as a good meal. — JIM DINE
1935–

Abstract qualities of design are essential to the value of a work, but to me of equal importance is the psychological human element. If both abstract and human elements are welded together in a work, it must have a fuller, deeper meaning. — HENRY MOORE
1898–1986

Yet if I believe I have found a great deal, then logically I must conclude that there still remains a great deal to be found by other painters; and they will find it. — PAUL GAUGUIN
1848–1903

My primary subject is the governing character of the light. . . . Appearances are always changing, I change. It is not possible to 'copy' a reality that is in flux. I take from that reality; I choose to see what I will, and that choice comes from an attitude toward painting and an attitude toward the things I am painting.

— JANET FISH
1938–

SUBJECT MATTER

My work is purely autobiographical. It's about myself and my surroundings. It is an attempt at a record.

— LUCIAN FREUD
1922–

I think it is important to be autobiographical. What I try to do in my work is explore myself in physical terms—to explain something in terms of my own sensibilities.

— JIM DINE
1935–

If the alphabet is A to Z, I want to move with it all the way, not only from A to C. For me, all the doors are open. One can't stop growing, though it takes enormous energy to keep growing and it is painful. Yet I have never been able to understand the artist whose image never changes.

— LEE KRASNER
1908–1983

Any incentive to paint is as good as any other. There is no poor subject.
— ROBERT RAUSCHENBERG
1925–

SUFFERING & PAIN

I have suffered great sorrow. . . . God willed it so.
— MICHELANGELO BUONARROTI
1475–1564

An artist must eat sparingly and give up a normal way of life.
— PIERRE AUGUSTE RENOIR
1841–1919

For freedom to paint as I please I have had to sacrifice comfort
and security and worldly pleasures. . . . — ALICE NEEL
1900–1984

I consciously choose the dog's path through life. I shall be poor;
I shall be a painter. . . . — VINCENT VAN GOGH
1853–1890

. . . it is clear that it was the great love of things and of people
and the incredible suffering of Van Gogh that made his art
possible and his insanity inevitable. — BEN SHAHN
1898–1969

Of course I suffer. Who doesn't? But I don't feel I've become a
better artist because of my suffering, but because of my willpower,
and the way that I have worked on myself. — FRANCIS BACON
1909–1992

Until the age of 50 I had all the worries of poverty.
— AUGUSTE RODIN
1840–1917

He who strives will never enjoy this life peacefully.
— PAUL KLEE
1879–1940

SUFFERING & PAIN

I am a great artist and I know it. It's because I am that I have
endured such sufferings. — PAUL GAUGUIN
1848–1903

I believe that the personality of the artist develops and asserts
itself through the struggles it has to go through when pitted
against other personalities. — HENRI MATISSE
1869–1954

[Artists] have their ups and downs . . . for a while everything
you do is wonderful or you think it is, then you slide down . . .
pulling yourself up again is the most important part of your life. — MILTON RESNICK
1917–

I've never learned to live comfortably. Comfort is an unnatural
state for me. The point is, I think that life is violent and most
people turn away from that side of it in an attempt to live a life
that is screened. But I think they are merely fooling themselves. — FRANCIS BACON
1909–1992

No amount of bodily suffering . . . would seem for me too
great a price for the pleasure of being in a country where one
could have some art advantages. — MARY CASSATT
1844–1926

This painting, this work that you mourn for, is the cause of
many griefs and many troubles. — BERTHE MORISOT
1841–1895

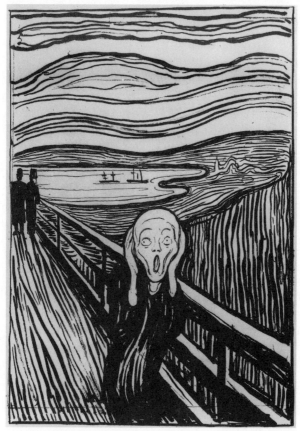

The Scream ▪ *Edvard Munch*
Lithograph, 13.9" x 9.8", 1895, courtesy of the Epstein Family Collection.

I was walking along a path with two friends, the sun was setting. I felt a breath of melancholy. Suddenly the sky turned blood-red. I stopped and leant against the railing, deathly tired, looking out across flaming clouds that hung like blood and a sword over the deep blue fjord and town. My friends walked on. I stood there trembling with anxiety and felt a great, infinite scream pass through nature.
— EDVARD MUNCH
1863–1944

TALENT

I dare affirm that any artist . . . who has nothing singular, eccentric, or at least reputed to be so, in his person, will never become a superior talent.
— MICHELANGELO BUONARROTI
1475–1564

Talent does not declare itself in an instant. It is not at the first attempt that one has the honesty to admit one's inabilities. How many attempts, now happy, now unhappy! . . . He who has not felt the difficulties of his art does nothing that counts.
— JEAN-BAPTIST-SIMÉON CHARDIN
1699–1779

Perhaps I have no talent, but all vanity aside—I do not believe that anyone makes an artistic attempt, no matter how small, without having a little—or there are many fools.
— PAUL GAUGUIN
1848–1903

The only amateurs are the people who do bad paintings.
— ÉDOUARD MANET
1832–1883

Skill is almost always fatal to feelings: the hand's dexterity . . . gives the artist too much freedom: he no longer thinks the picture clearly; the ability to render it with facility or short cuts seduces him and leads him to mannerism.
— EUGÈNE DELACROIX
1798–1863

In my opinion, art or talent, for an artist, is merely a means of applying his personal faculties to the idea and the things of the period in which he lives.
— GUSTAVE COURBET
1819–1877

It would be a mistake to ascribe this creative power to an inborn talent. In art, the genuine creator is not just a gifted being, but a person who has succeeded in arranging for their appointed end, a complex of activities, of which the work is the outcome.
— HENRI MATISSE
1869–1954

If you have a gift, it is your halo and your cross. There is no choice. You are what you are, what you have been born. And what is inherent in that condition is the loneliness that goes with it.
— HELEN FRANKENTHALER
1928–

I would never consciously trade awkwardness for elegance.
— RICHARD DIEBENKORN
1922–1993

Looking back on my work today, I think the best I have done grew out of things deeply felt, the worst from a pride in mere talent.
— DIEGO RIVERA
1886–1957

TALENT

I am doubtful of any talent, so whatever I choose to be, will be accomplished only by long study and work. . . . As to what I would like to be, it is difficult to say. An artist of some kind. If nothing else I shall always study the Arts.

— JACKSON POLLOCK
1912–1956

If Picasso had spent his whole life making drawings and portraits capable of standing up beside Ingres's—which he amply demonstrated that he could do—he'd have ended up another Augustus John, a man who did no more than follow the bent of his talent, and not Picasso.

— FRANZ KLINE
1910–1962

I've not been cursed with talent, which could be a great inhibitor.

— ROBERT RAUSCHENBERG
1925–

ASTE

I prefer the still primitive art of Olympus to that of the
Parthenon. It is the most beautiful thing that I have seen; it is
more beautiful than anything else in the world. . . . If I had
lived in the sixth century I should have found happiness in
working with these men. — ARISTIDE MAILLOL
1861–1944

It is rarely other than the lowest type of arts, whether in painting
or in poetry or in music, which naturally pleases the multitude.
— JEAN-AUGUSTE-DOMINIQUE INGRES
1780–1867

Taste is the best judge. It is rare. Art only addresses itself to an
excessively small number of individuals.
— PAUL CÉZANNE
1839–1906

*Only the work of art itself can raise the
standard of taste.* — DIEGO RIVERA
1886–1957

But as I see it, the most corrupt art is the sentimental. . . .
— CAMILLE PISSARRO
1830–1903

Taste for things of the past evolves, doesn't it? What was a
masterpiece a hunded years ago is no longer so today.
— ALBERTO GIACOMETTI
1901–1966

TASTE

The vulgar will see nothing but chaos, disorder, and incorrectness.
— JAMES ENSOR
1860–1949

I *force myself to contradict myself, so as to avoid conforming to my own taste.*
— MARCEL DUCHAMP
1887–1968

Of course it's subjective. It is for everyone and has always been so. . . . When you look at art made by other people, you see what you need to see in it.
— ALBERTO GIACOMETTI
1901–1966

A painter's tastes must grow out of what so obsesses him in life that he never has to ask himself what it is suitable for him to do in art. . . . The painter's obsession with his subject is all that he needs to drive him to work.
— LUCIAN FREUD
1922–

He [the artist] must try to raise the level of taste of the masses, not debase himself to the level of unformed and impoverished taste.
— DIEGO RIVERA
1886–1957

TECHNIQUE & PROCESS

The artist must know the manner whereby to convince others
of the truthfulness of his lies. — PABLO PICASSO
1881–1973

Techniques vary; art stays the same: it is a translation of nature
at once forceful and sensitive. — CLAUDE MONET
1840–1926

The most skilled hand is never anything but the servant of the
mind. . . . Even if the professional schools should succeed in
producing skilled workers trained in the technique of their
craft, nothing could be done with them if they had no ideal.
— PIERRE AUGUSTE RENOIR
1841–1919

For after all the questions of material, of technique, even of the
preparation of the canvas, are of the least importance. They can
always be remedied can't they . . . you can be precise if you care
about it; with practice the craft will come almost of itself, in
spite of you and all the more easily if you think of something
besides technique. — PAUL GAUGUIN
1848–1903

*The artist should fear to become the slave
of detail. He should strive to express his
thought and not the surface of it.*
— ALBERT PINKHAM RYDER
1847–1917

TECHNIQUE & PROCESS

I don't begin by drawing on the canvas. I make marks, and
then I use all sorts of things to work with: old brooms, old
sweaters, and all kinds of peculiar tools and materials. . . . I
paint to excite myself, and make something for myself.

— FRANCIS BACON
1909–1992

Clever people can copy the handwriting of an artist—it's like
forging a person's signature. One mustn't let technique be the
consciously important thing. It should be at the service of
expressing the form.

— HENRY MOORE
1898–1986

To be interested solely in technique would be a very superficial
thing to me. If I have an emotion, before I die, that's deeper
than any emotion that I've ever had, then I will paint a more
powerful picture that will have nothing to do with just
technique, but will go beyond it.

— ANDREW WYETH
1917–

In photography, as with most things in life, there is a natural
tendency to want to establish a clearly defined procedure.
However, when the entire process becomes a prescribed ritual
that does not allow for spontaneous variations and reactions,
the vitality of the medium and our relation to it suffers.

— JERRY UELSMANN
1934–

When you begin a picture, you often make some pretty discoveries. You must be on guard against these. Destroy the thing, do it over several times. In each destroying of a beautiful discovery the artist does not really suppress it, but rather transforms it, condenses it, makes it more substantial.

— PABLO PICASSO
1881–1973

The notion that a painter suddenly imagines a composition expressive of his feelings and straightaway puts it down is untrue. He begins with a general idea. . . . He proceeds by trial and error . . . the process was one of exploration as well as expression.

— JOYCE CAREY
1888–1957

One should work the same subject ten times, a hundred times over. Nothing in art should look accidental, not even movement.

— EDGAR DEGAS
1834–1917

If you work on a little bit of unworked clay, it gets to look bigger. The more you work on it, the bigger it gets.

— ALBERTO GIACOMETTI
1901–1966

The brush is a more powerful and rapid tool than the point or the stump . . . the main thing that the brush secures is the instant grasp of the grand construction of a figure.

— THOMAS EAKINS
1844–1916

A picture used to be a sum of additions. In my case a picture is a sum of destruction. I do a picture—then I destroy it. In the end, though, nothing is lost: the red I took away from one place turns up somewhere else. — PABLO PICASSO
1881–1973

It's when you've found out how to do certain things, that it's time to stop doing them, because what's missing is that you're not including the risk. The fact is, risk is essential to me.
— ROBERT RAUSCHENBERG
1925–

I throw an awful lot of paint on to things, and I don't know what is going to happen to it. . . . I throw it with my hand. I just squeeze it into my hand and throw it on. . . . I can only hope that the throwing of the paint on to the ready-made image or half-made image will either re-form the image or that I will be able to manipulate this paint further into—anyway, for me—a greater intensity. — FRANCIS BACON
1909–1992

The great painters separated form and color as a means to realization. They did it by underpainting the form in semineutral colors and bringing the sculptured low relief into plastic existence by superimposed color glazes.
— JOHN SLOAN
1871–1951

So for the painter, when he has his new, his magic landscape in front of him: he has to fix it down. And at once he is up against enormous difficulties. He has only his paints and brushes, and a flat piece of canvas with which to convey a sensation, a feeling about a three-dimensional world. He has somehow to translate an intuition from real objects into a formal and ideal arrangement of colors and shapes . . . he has a job that requires thought, skill, and a lot of experience.

— JOYCE CAREY
1888–1957

I have learned from experience that it is useful to begin by drawing one's picture clearly on a virgin canvas, first having noted the desired effect on a white or gray paper, and then to do the picture section by section, as immediately finished as one can, so that when it has all been covered there is very little to retouch.

— JEAN-BAPTIST-CAMILLE COROT
1796–1875

I have gradually changed from using preliminary drawings for my sculpture to working from the beginning in three dimensions. That is, I first make a maquette for any idea that I have for sculpture. The maquette is only three or four inches in size, and I can hold it in my hand, turning it over to look at it from above, underneath and in fact from every angle. Thus, from the very beginning I am working and thinking in three dimensions.

— HENRY MOORE
1898–1986

TECHNIQUE & PROCESS

I first block in the chosen scene or object with broad brushstrokes. Then I begin using brushes of diminishing sizes that are gradually reduced to the smallest sable point . . . that's what takes forever—closing in on the minutest detail and still have it be part of the whole.

— CATHERINE MURPHY
1946–

I develop the whole image as faithfully as possible, without expression, without editorializing, without fancy brushwork. Everything is limited by the lighting, walls and other conditions of my studio.

— PHILIP PEARLSTEIN
1924–

I always do an acrylic underpainting because I find it very easy to work with, because you can make a lot of changes. . . . But it is very difficult to get a real finish with acrylic. It's not so much the blending, but just the colors; they don't seem to have the brilliance the oil paints have, the depth which you can get with oils.

— RICHARD ESTES
1932–

It is not enough for a painter to be a clever craftsman; he must love to 'caress' his canvas, too.

— PIERRE AUGUSTE RENOIR
1841–1919

The conflict for realization is what makes art, not its certainty, nor its technique or material. I do not look for total success. . . . I will not change an error if it feels right, for the error is more human than perfection. — DAVID SMITH
1906–1965

I only want to do simple, very simple art . . . with no other thought in mind but to render, the way a child would, the concepts formed in my brain and to do this with the aid of nothing but the primitive means of art, the only means that are good and true. . . . — PAUL GAUGUIN
1848–1903

I approach painting in the same sense as one approaches drawing: that is, it's direct. I don't work from drawings, I don't make sketches and drawings and color sketches into a final painting. — JACKSON POLLOCK
1912–1956

I don't want a painting to be just an expression of my personality. I feel it ought to be much better than that. And I'm opposed to the whole idea of conception—execution—of getting an idea for a picture and then carrying it out. I've always felt as though, whatever I've used and whatever I've done, the method was always closer to a collaboration with materials than to any kind of conscious manipulation and control. — ROBERT RAUSCHENBERG
1925–

TRUTH & LIES

Truth exists. Only lies are invented.

— GEORGES BRAQUE
1882–1963

'Art' is the same word as 'artifice,' that is to say, something deceitful. It must succeed in giving the impression of nature by false means.
— EDGAR DEGAS
1834–1917

I think a quality of artificiality must be retained in a work of art, since, after all, the reality of art is not to be confused with that of the outer world. Art, it must be remembered, is artifice, or a creative undertaking, the primary function of which is to add to our existing conception of reality.

— ROMARE BEARDEN
1914–

I have tried to do what is true and not ideal.

— HENRI DE TOULOUSE-LAUTREC
1864–1901

I've decided that art is a habit-forming drug. That's all it is, for the artist, for the collector, for anybody connected with it. Art has absolutely no existence as veracity, as truth.

— MARCEL DUCHAMP
1887–1968

People believe photographs. From childhood we are taught to believe them. . . . So when you have a photograph like mine, with all the fidelity of a traditional image, yet at the same time presenting another kind of realism—a kind of magic realism— then it leads you to question what you believe. It makes you think.
— JERRY UELSMANN
1934–

Not honesty of structure, but the appearance of honesty, is what we are after.
— PHILIP JOHNSON
1900–1964

'Objectification' is not the final aim of art. For there are greater things than the object. The greatest thing is the human mind. . . . My paintings are always images of my whole psychic makeup. You cannot deny yourself.
— HANS HOFMANN
1880–1966

From the point of view of art, there are no concrete or abstract forms, but only forms which are more or less convincing lies.
— PABLO PICASSO
1881–1973

I hardly need to abstract things for each object is unreal enough already, so unreal that I can only make it real by means of painting.
— MAX BECKMANN
1884–1950

The mind's eye in its infinity of radiations and not optical vision of necessity hold the key to truth.

— ARSHILE GORKY
1904–1948

That which is ugly in art is that which is false and artificial— that which aims at being pretty or even beautiful instead of being expressive.

— AUGUSTE RODIN
1840–1917

Drawing is not a natural act. You've got this flatness and you have to learn to lie about it.

— WAYNE THIEBAUD
1920–

A picture is something which requires as much knavery, trickery and deceit as the perpetration of a crime.

— EDGAR DEGAS
1834–1917

I have made my own reality. I'm not seeking the concept truth. . . . A truth isn't a truth to me, a lie isn't a lie. . . . And if a so called truth can destroy me, the hell with it. I cling to my own standards as much as I can.

— LOUISE NEVELSON
1900–1988

Art is a lie that makes us realize the truth.

— PABLO PICASSO
1881–1973

WORKING & WORK HABITS

Painting is manual labor, no different from any other; it can be done well or poorly. — GEORGE GROSZ
1893–1959

Why do people think artists are special? It's just another job. — ANDY WARHOL
1927?–1987

For the essential thing about the work of art is that it is work, and very hard work too. — JOYCE CAREY
1888–1957

Things are not difficult to make; what is difficult is putting ourselves in the state of mind to make them. — CONSTANTIN BRANCUSI
1876–1957

In art intentions are not sufficient. . . . What one does is what counts and not what one has intentions of doing. — PABLO PICASSO
1881–1973

Very few people know how to work. Inspiration, everybody has inspiration, that's just hot air. — BEATRICE WOOD
1895–1998

Industry in art is a necessity—not a virtue—and any evidence of the same, in the production, is a blemish, not a quality; a proof, not of achievement, but of absolutely insufficent work, for work alone will efface the footsteps of work.

— JAMES ABBOT McNEILL WHISTLER
1834–1903

The work of a man is the explanation of the man.

— PAUL GAUGUIN
1848–1903

We are not merely the executors of our work; we live our work.

— PABLO PICASSO
1881–1973

Some people would say that it is not human for a woman or for a man to put their work before everything. But I don't see how you can create and not have the feeling that it is the most important, all-consuming thing.   — GRACE HARTIGAN
1922–

I try to begin working with no preconceived ideas.

— JERRY UELSMANN
1934–

When you work you learn something about what you are doing and you develop habits and procedures out of what you're doing.

— JASPER JOHNS
1930–

I get up, six in the morning. And I wear cotton clothes so that I can sleep in them or I can work in them—I don't want to waste time. I go to the studio, and usually I put in pretty much of a big day. . . . Sometimes I could work two, three days and not sleep and I didn't pay any attention to food.

— LOUISE NEVELSON
1900–1988

I found one had to do some work every day, even at midnight, because either you're professional or you're not.
— DAME BARBARA HEPWORTH
1903–1975

I get up early and ease into the day for about an hour. Then I start working. There are a lot of tricks you have to keep playing on yourself to keep at it because every time you hit a problem you want to walk away.
— JANET FISH
1938–

I like to start working when it's almost too late . . . when nothing else helps . . . when my sense of efficiency is exhausted. It's then that I find myself in another state, quite outside of myself, and when that happens, there's such a joy! It's an incredible high, and things just start flowing, and you have no idea of the source.

— ROBERT RAUSCHENBERG
1925–

It seems that whatever you do . . . the residue takes a form, and you develop insights that feed back into your thinking and becomes like new habits, new attachments.

— JASPER JOHNS
1930–

And to get the work done that I must do, one has to work in isolation and not be readily disturbed. . . . I don't have daily newspapers, and I like to feel when I get up in the morning my attention is fixed on the work I am going to do.

— REG BUTLER
1913–1981

When I can't work, or when I have a problem, I immediately start to draw. In order to disengage myself, to try to find a solution. . . . They are drawings that I do for myself; I don't do them for others. . . . My drawings are purely functional.

— JEAN TINGUELY
1925–

For me it would be worthwhile to work even if there were no outcome for others, simply for my own vision, my vision of the external world, of people. — ALBERTO GIACOMETTI
1901–1966

My contact sheets become a kind of visual diary of all the things I have seen and experienced with my camera. They contain the seeds from which my images grow.

— JERRY UELSMANN
1934–

I have no conscious premise while working of why I am working, what it is I am making, or whom it is for. . . . I'm a revolutionary, and hope always to remain one. An arrogant independence to create is my only motivation.

— DAVID SMITH
1906–1965

*I*t is the outcome of work which makes the greatest contribution to creation. If we never arrive at astonishment about our work, we never create new forms.

— PABLO PICASSO
1881–1973

I was always conscious of the difficulty of everything, and I thought that by willpower and concentration I could somehow force my way. That simply using my eyes and my willpower I could overcome what I felt was my lack of natural ability. I didn't feel that I had no ability, but I felt that the only way I could work properly was by using the absolute maximum of observation and maximum concentration that I could possibly muster.

— LUCIAN FREUD
1922–

It is very hard work to turn out anything that looks like a good painting.

— GEORGIA O'KEEFFE
1887–1986

Art is not the fashion industry where you market something new each year. I work very slowly, by myself . . . and I don't analyze my artistic impulse. If you analyze, you eliminate chance. Art is about mystery.

— MARISOL
1930–

Nothing can be rushed. It must grow, it should grow of itself . . .
— PAUL KLEE
1879–1940

I go to work as others rush to see their mistresses, and when I leave, I take back with me to my solitude, or in the midst of the distractions that I pursue, a charming memory that does not in the least resemble the troubled pleasure of lovers.
— EUGÈNE DELACROIX
1796–1863

I paint with the stubbornness I need for living, and I've found that all painters who love their art do the same.
— SUZANNE VALADON
1865–1938

The words 'work' and 'art' are synonyms.

> — ANONYMOUS

I work every day. I work all day, I've never had a holiday. It's all I really want to do. It's what I'm here for. . . . More and more, I'm just so grateful I was born an artist.

> — JIM DINE
> *1935–*

I need to work to feel well.

> — ÉDOUARD MANET
> *1832–1883*

It will be useful too if he quit work often and take some relaxation; judgment will be clearer upon his return.

> — LEONARDO DA VINCI
> *1452–1519*

The important thing is to do, and nothing else; be what it may.

> — PABLO PICASSO
> *1881–1973*

ABOUT THE EDITOR

CLINT BROWN has exhibited his art work for more than twenty-five years. He is currently a professor of art at Oregon State University and was a Fulbright exchange teacher in Great Britain. He is the author of *Drawing from Life,* a figure drawing text now in its second edition, published by Harcourt Brace. He received his bachelor of fine arts degree from the University of Wisconsin in Milwaukee and his master of fine arts degree from the University of Southern California.

▮NDEX